The Durham Village Book

THE VILLAGES OF BRITAIN SERIES

Other counties in this series include:

Avon
Bedfordshire
Berkshire
Buckinghamshire
Cambridgeshire
Cheshire
Cleveland
Cornwall
Cumbria
Derbyshire
Devon
Dorset
Essex
Gloucestershire
Hampshire
Herefordshire
Hertfordshire
Kent
Lancashire
Leicestershire & Rutland
Lincolnshire
Middlesex
Norfolk
Northamptonshire
Nottinghamshire
Oxfordshire
Powys Montgomeryshire
Shropshire
Somerset
Staffordshire
Suffolk
Surrey
East Sussex
West Sussex
Warwickshire
West Midlands
Wiltshire
Worcestershire
East Yorkshire
North Yorkshire
South & West Yorkshire

Most are published in conjunction with County Federations of Women's Institutes

The Durham Village Book

Compiled by the Durham
Federation of Women's Institutes from notes
and illustrations sent by Institutes in the County

Published jointly by
Countryside Books, Newbury
and the DFWI, Durham

First Published 1992

Countryside Books
3 Catherine Road
Newbury, Berkshire

ISBN 1 85306 198 0

Cover photograph of Newbiggin
taken by Kathleen Teward

Produced through MRM Associates Ltd, Reading
Typeset by Acorn Bookwork, Salisbury
Printed in England by J. W. Arrowsmith Ltd., Bristol

Foreword

We proudly present for your enjoyment our very own publication, 'The Durham Village Book'.

Our grateful thanks go to all the W.I. members who have contributed to it. As authors or illustrators, their stories and anecdotes, along with factual history, bring out the true flavour and atmosphere of our unique county, which stretches from the moors of Teesdale and Weardale to the sea.

We hope this book will become a valued companion in your leisure time whether by the fireside, or exploring our beautiful county.

Evelyn Stevenson
County Chairman

Acknowledgements

The Durham Federation of Women's Institutes would like to thank all members who have worked so hard to provide material and illustrations for this book. We are grateful to Mr David Price for Witton Le Wear and Mr Emery for Waterhouses. Finally, a special thank you to Beth Carr who co-ordinated the project.

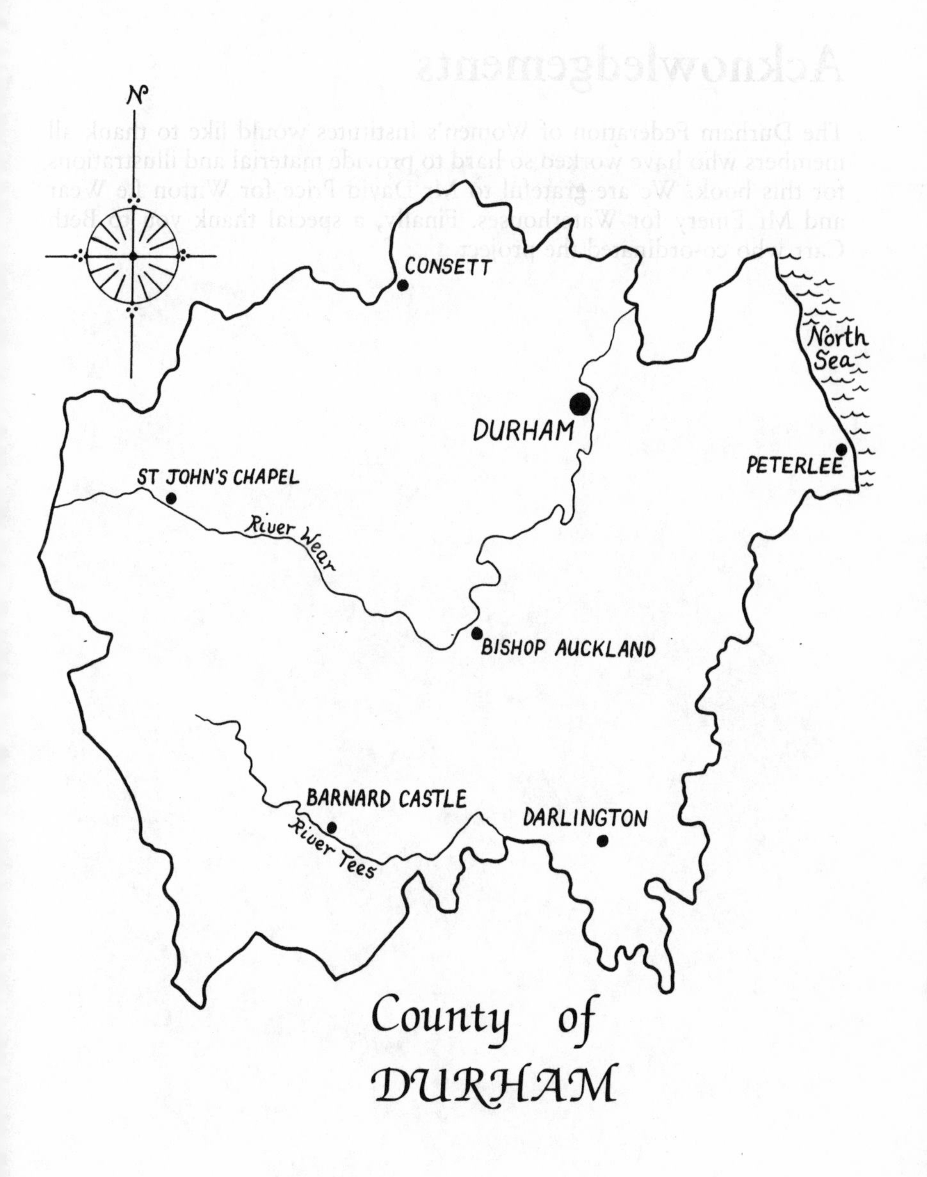
N
CONSETT
North Sea
DURHAM
PETERLEE
ST JOHN'S CHAPEL
River Wear
BISHOP AUCKLAND
BARNARD CASTLE
River Tees
DARLINGTON
County of
DURHAM

Annfield Plain

The area in which Annfield Plain developed was known as the Lanchester Common when much of the land was rough pasture or woodland. It would seem from history that the earliest buildings were probably those of sheep farmers as it is known that farms of 600 or more sheep existed in the 1500s and the 1600s. At the same time shallow mines or pits were being developed on the west side of Pontop Pike when it was realised that coal could be used for heating and melting metals instead of wood. Mining enterprise came into being in the late 1600s and early 1700s. The earliest house of note, Annfield House, was erected on the summit of the Loud Hill sometime during the period 1710 to 1750. Greencroft Hall and Tower were built in 1670 and the estate bordered the southern side of the road from Maiden Law to Greencroft.

Mining became the principal industry with many shallow mines being sunk in the area notably at Greencroft, Pontop, East Pontop and Hare Law. The population in 1801 was thought to be in the region of 300 to 500. Growth of mining brought about one of the most important developments in the laying of the track of the Stanhope and Tyne Railway from Stanhope to South Shields a distance of 33¾ miles. The railway became operative in 1834 and was crucial in the growth of the Derwent Iron works at Consett after 1840. Coal from the surrounding collieries was transported by this railway line which ran through Oxhill, Stanley, Stella Gill and then on to South Shields via Washington.

The village had three names – originally Anfield, then Annfield Plane following the advent of the Stanhope and Tyne Railway in 1834 – 'the Plane' being the level ground between Annfield Plane, Oxhill and Stanley. In 1856 the name's spelling was changed to 'Annfield Plain' which has remained to this day.

It was about this time that the first building of houses took place in Annfield Plain when 60 houses for miners at the Pontop Colliery were erected on a site now occupied by Granville Avenue, Front Street and Railway Gardens in 1838–39. More mines were opened in the mid 1800s notably the South Derwent Colliery (1872) or 'Billy' pit as it was known, The Morrison North and South Pits (1869). These mines were deeper than the early mines, some of which were now deepened or second shafts sunk. Alongside this activity coke ovens were built notably by the Pontop Windsor Colliery (200 Ovens), East Pontop Colliery (80 ovens), East Castle Colliery (74 ovens), South Derwent Collieries known as the 'Billy' pit and the 'Cresswell Bankfort' or 'Hutton' pit (60 ovens). Mining and its by-products created most of the employment in the area. The village had moved from a hamlet in the 18th century to be a comparatively large centre of population. The village became to a large extent self-supporting having a brewery, a mill, a candle factory, a school, a Church of England, a Primitive Methodist Chapel and other Methodist Chapels at Catchgate. The Crown and Thistle Inn opened in 1817 being a conversion of a dwelling house the origins of which by the deeds is 1670. The Smith's Arms began in 1850 and the Railway Tavern in Annfield Plain is shown on very old photographs of Annfield Plain and whilst it bears the date 1899 on its frontage it was in existence as a building many years before that time. Together with the 'Queen Victoria Public House' now known as the Queen's Head Hotel they are both shown as such on the earliest Ordnance Survey map of 1857.

A small group of men took it upon themselves to foster the idea of a Co-operative Store for which purpose they sought the advice of their neighbours, Tantobie Co-operative Society, which led to the establishment of Annfield Plain Industrial Co-operative Society in a small shop formerly situated on a site where the Democratic Club and Institute is now built. The shop was occupied on 13th May, 1870 and opened for business on the 17th May, 1870. The Society moved into newly built premises in 1873 and gradually expanded, rebuilding its own premises in 1925 and establishing branches in Lanchester, Esh Winning, Medomsley, Sacriston, Dipton, Catchgate and Durham.

Most outstanding among the local notables were two pioneers in early mining, John Curr and John Buddle. John Curr and John Buddle were born in West Kyo, part of Annfield Plain. In 1765 the former went as steward to the Duke of Norfolk's collieries in Sheffield and being in touch with the iron industry he invented in 1776 metal tramplates and also four-wheeled bogies the prototype of the modern mine tub. 1790 saw him introduce cast iron rails. He was so well thought of for his inventions that 'The Pitman's Pay' printed a little rhyme – 'God bless the man with peace and plenty, Who first invented metal plates; Draw out his days to five times twenty and slide him through the Heavenly Gates.'

John Buddle was born in Kyo in 1773. His father was a schoolmaster in Chester-le-Street. John was given a good education especially in mathematics. He was first Manager of Greenside Colliery and later Wallsend. His improvements in mining techniques led to him being recognised as a consultant on mining matters so much that the Institute of Mining Engineers in Newcastle has a life size painting of him and a bronze medal bearing his image is periodically given to those who make outstanding contributions to mining.

The social life of Annfield Plain in the 1870s and 1880s developed within the confines of the village. There were no trains until 1894 and, of course, no cars or buses. The first cyclist was said to be Mr Hinds, headmaster of Hare Law School and this is alleged to have taken place in 1865. Communication with the outside world was by means of horsedrawn brake (a long cart) which visited Newcastle twice per week on Wednesday Market Day and Saturdays. The fare was one shilling (5p) each way. Some owners of brakes were Oxleys, Edwards and Holmes in the area. A trip to the seaside by brake often took about four hours. The brakes were drawn by three horses and the passengers had to walk up all hills.

Annfield Plain had a cricket team and the first cricket field in the village was on land now occupied by South View Gardens and the former site of the bakery and the dairy. The cricket field was known as the 'Store' field and was probably used for grazing the many horses owned by the Annfield Plain Co-operative Industrial Society which were employed in hauling delivery carts and mobile shops selling hardware products and greengrocery. Other sports or pastimes were pigeon racing, dog racing (greyhounds) and each weekend saw some event to provide entertainment for those not working. Quoits was a game which attracted many. There was at South Pontop (Greencroft) the annual visit of the circus usually Swallow's or Gunnet's. This took place in the middle of the 'high square' at the Lizzie or South Pontop. Wild beast shows were held. Football became very popular and originally took place on a field behind the Annfield Plain Board School. Later football took place on a field which had formerly been the site of the 'Lizzie' Squares owned by U. A. Ritson. At the present time (1991) the club functions in the Wearside League.

Horse racing and foot-running were held in the 'Store' field on St Leger Day when a local businessman, Mr Strawbridge, organised various events such as the Greencroft Steeplechase, the Annfield Plain Flat Race and the Catchgate Stakes, prizes being £5 first and £1 second. Horse racing is said to have been ended in 1885, following missions held by Methodists when speakers spoke out against drink and gambling at the race meetings.

It is recorded that the All-England Pigeon Shooting contest was held at Annfield Plain on 26th January, 1889.

Kyo Flower Show was held annually until the middle to late 1920s on land approximately where the Catchgate R.A.O.B. Club now stands. Usually an invitation was extended to a well-known brass band to attend the show and give a concert on the show-field on the Saturday evening of the show. As well as the local bands such as South Moor, the South Derwent and the Morrison, there were others one of which was the Wallsend Rising Sun Colliery Band under the conductorship of Mr Robert Humble, a former baritone player with the South Derwent Band and the world famous St Hilda Colliery Band of South Shields and a native of Annfield Plain.

As well as the numerous sports and pastimes there are a number of organisations following their own particular pursuits e.g. a horticultural club, various allotment associations and many more. The Annfield Plain Community Centre was established in the former Greencroft School and has a number of organisations such as a Ladies' Club, a Billiards and Snooker Group and an 'Over 60's' Club.

The Annfield Plain area has always shown a keen interest in music and drama. This has been shown by the formation of the Annfield Plain Gleemen in 1903 and which has continued up to the present time. Many will remember the Eastertide concerts in the Methodist Churches, notably St John's and the Central Methodist Church (or Primitive Methodist Church formerly) and also Catchgate Methodist Church. One must not forget also the colliery brass bands which gave concerts in the bandstand of the Annfield Plain Park.

In the early 1970s the goods station together with other property on the frontage of Station Road was bought by the North Eastern Co-operative Society and a new Super Store built. The former buildings of the Co-operative Store were demolished and replaced by a complex, housing a school psychological centre, flats for the elderly and a care section for those of the elderly unable to care for themselves. Part of the former buildings have been re-erected at the Beamish Museum. The last coal mine in the area was the Morrison Busty Colliery situated on the Lanchester road south of the former Morrison North and South pits. This closed in 1973 having been sunk between 1922 and 1927.

In an effort to help the employment situation arising out of the closure of mines etc. the firm of Ransome and Marles (later Ransome, Hoffman and Pollard) from Peterborough established itself in a large factory built on the Greencroft to Maiden Law Road. This factory produced ball-bearings for industry generally and the car manufacturing industry in particular. The factory was opened in 1953 and closed in 1981/82. This was a heavy blow since about 2000 local people had been employed in the factory. Various other smaller factories manufacturing clothing, gloves etc. set up in premises formerly used as Miners' Halls (New Kyo in particular), the former mill at Catchgate, the cemetery chapel at Hare Law, but industry became more organised by the establishment of industrial estates at Hare Law, Greencroft and Maiden Law.

Barnard Castle

The history of Barnard Castle is dominated by the Baliol Family. For in 1066 William of Normandy conquered England, at the battle of Hastings.

In his retinue was Guido de Baliol, whose name became changed to Guy Baliol and for his loyalty and help through the years was rewarded by being granted the Forests of Teesdale and Marwood, and the Lordship of Middleton and Gainford.

The Castle, a small fortification enclosed in the inner Bailey was probably erected in the late 11th century by Guy Baliol. It took its name from Bernard Baliol, his heir and nephew. It was Bernard who built the Great Wall enclosure and established the town outside the Castle. His son Bernard Baliol II, granted and endowed to the townsfolk the land freehold and so the market town of Barnard Castle began to grow. John Baliol and his wife Devorguilla, became famous as founders of Baliol College at Oxford. John Baliol later became Regent of Scotland through the rights of his wife, who was the daughter of the Lord of Galloway.

His mother was Agnes-De-Valencia, niece to Henry III of England. In about the 14th year of the King's reign John Baliol founded a Hospital in Newgate dedicated to 'John the Baptist' and endowed it with land. The Deeds and Endowment were lost, but the nominations of the Hospital's Master, for many years remained with the Lord Chancellor in London.

Many years later the Castle and land was bestowed on Anne Neville, daughter of Richard Neville, Earl of Warwick known as 'The King-maker', as part of her dowry when she married Richard Duke of

Gloucester. The Castle and Estates were in active occupation when he became King Richard III and it is understood that he enlarged the buildings and strengthened the defence. King Richard's Crest 'The White Boar Passant' can be seen on the wall of the Castle and also on a couple of houses.

Barnard Castle played its part in the Rising of the North. After the rising was defeated, The Earl of Northumberland was hung, drawn and quartered and his head spiked on the main Gateway of York. The Earl of Westmorland fled to the North East and ended in Flanders, where he subsisted on a small pension allowed him by the King of Spain.

Curfew began in Barnard Castle by order of the Queen Elizabeth I. Apparently she stated that the townspeople and the Dales would never plot against the Crown again. This started the ringing of the Church Bell, at 7.55pm until 8pm prompt, with townspeople off the streets and in their homes with closed doors and no public meetings. This tradition was carried out until the 2nd World War and discontinued in peace.

In reference to Agnes-De-Valencia, when her husband died she had his heart removed from his body, embalmed and placed in a leather pouch, so wherever she travelled her 'Sweetheart' went with her.

She travelled to Scotland where her son became Regent of Scotland. She died in Scotland and her sweetheart was buried with her at Sweetheart Abbey.

Today Barnard Castle sits picturesquely perched over the peat brown waters of the Tees flowing east to industrial Teesside, forming the boundary between Durham and its Yorkshire neighbour until 1974.

In the main street stands the Butter market built in 1747 with what was once the administrative headquarters of the town and courts were held. And not far from here is Blagraves House, once an inn where Oliver Cromwell partook of mulled wine and cake. The house has a projecting gable with leaded windows and four small figures of men playing musical instruments.

Not far from the Butter Market lies the King's Head hotel where Charles Dickens stayed on his foray North in 1838 to collect material for *Nicholas Nickleby* and write about Dotheboys Hall.

Galgate is at the top of the market place and follows the line of the Roman road from Bowes to Binchester near Bishop Auckland.

Not far from Barnard Castle lies the beautiful Palladian style country house of Rokeby which was the setting for Sir Walter Scott's ballad Rokeby – a fabulous collection of 18th century embroidered pictures can be seen at this former home of Sir Thomas Robinson.

Sir Humphrey Davy once lived at Rokeby.

Egglestone Abbey, a ruined Premonstratensian abbey dating from the 12th century and a quaint medieval pack horse bridge make the visit worth while.

Back in the town a visit to the Parish church has a raised Chancel – six steps above the nave. The black marble font was hewn from the bed of the Tees.

A memorial to a former Baron of the Exchequer can be seen. He was Sir John Hullock, born in the town in 1767 – a once prominent lawyer who lived in Thorngate.

A memorial too to Captain Augustus Webb fatally wounded during the Charge of the Light Brigade, of the 'gallant sixhundred' at Balaclava.

Bowes Museum, built of local stone from Stainton and Streathlam by John Bowes and his French actress wife Countess Josephine Montalbo, a talented artist in her own right is one reason for visiting the capital of Teesdale.

The collection has been added to greatly over the years adding two Canaletto's to a priceless collection of national treasures. The exhibits include furniture, ceramics, textiles together with local geological items, and toys to delight any youngster are just some of the pleasures of the visit.

And you can buy a piece of cake made to the Queen Mother's recipe in the cafe!

Barningham

The village of Barningham, meaning 'the hamlet of BEORN'S people is situated in lower Teesdale, on the edge of the Pennines. Until 1974 it was in North Yorkshire. The houses are mainly built of sandstone and are situated either side of the east–west village street which rises west to the moors which stretch away to the horizon. Barnard Castle can be seen in the distance to the north. It is a farming area with a few farms still in and around the village. Farm hands and staff from the Big House, Barningham Park, used to live in most of the houses but now are mainly lived in by people working in Barnard Castle, Darlington and Teeside.

The church built in 1815 and restored in 1891 is a happy and well attended church. Nearby is 'The Hollies', a cottage which was once an inn called the 'Boot and Shoe'. An old sign dated 1715 was found in the house. Another old inn can be found up the village street, now called Elim Cottage situated opposite the Wesleyan Chapel. Formerly it was the 'Black Horse'. A leading Methodist gentleman thought it unsuitable to have a pub so near the chapel and had it converted into a house re-named Elim, a place named in the bible.

There was no special industry in Barningham but at Park View Thomas Binks (1737) the Barningham clockmaker, had his workshop at the back of the house. The next door cottage was used as a granary for the brewery which was housed in the outbuildings of Park View and the next cottage was a joiner's shop.

Newby House was built in the 1780s by George Newby as a Dotheboys Hall type school. He died in 1827 and was succeeded by Mr Thomas Grainger Coates who had a high reputation as School Master.

> 'They're clever folk do live at Barningham
> O'wd skewlmaster Coates is a boy for learning 'em'.

Barningham Park belongs to the Milbank family who have lived there for many years. There is a beautiful garden situated on a hill with a beck tumbling down. The garden is open to the public on some Sundays in the summer. The Milbanks built the village school which was in use until 1946 when Sir Frederick gave it to the village to be used as a village hall. He stipulated that children's sports should be held annually on the Saturday nearest June 16th. This is carried out and is one of the many uses made of the village green. The children play cricket, football, rounders and other games.

There is a quoits pitch where a thriving club plays matches and practises; a flourishing cricket club which has two teams for youngsters and two for adults, and a children's football club for both boys and girls. They have a successful team who play in league matches and do quite well.

In the old days there used to be resident in the village the rector, Methodist minister, schoolmaster, nurse, doctor, cobbler, joiner, stonemason and a shopkeeper, but now we only have a rector, a building firm, a nursery garden and two stonemasons, and of course a handyman.

Electricity was generated from a generator at the Park which lit five street lamps up the village street. Grandfather Brass lit the lamps at 5.30

p.m. each evening and put them out at 9.30 p.m. There was always a great rush by W.I. members after their meeting to get home before Mr Brass doused the lights. The mains electricity arrived in 1948 and now the street is lit with not very satisfactory yellow lights.

The fountain on the green, built in 1864, supplied water for the village for many years. It was superseded by handsome, iron stand pipes placed at convenient intervals up the village. Only three are now standing. Alas! the rest have been knocked over by cars.

The W.I., started in 1933 by Lady Milbank, was busy during the Second World War with 'make do and mend', knitting, egg collections etc. Some village ladies joined the land army, others went into the observer corp. The W.I. drama group was active, and much enjoyed by them if not always appreciated by the audience! They entertained in other villages, sometimes having to change in extraordinary places – once a coal house lit by one candle. There was also a church choir that sang in church and gave concerts round about, battling with all kinds of pianos. They competed in many tournaments and in 1923 won the Teesdale Music Festival Tournament. There is a shield in the Village Hall to prove it.

Now there is a church choir, called The 'Occasional Choir' who sing at Church Festivals and other special occasions. They also sing in Wycliffe and Hutton Magna Churches. One year they took part in the Wensleydale Tournament of Song and came first in one class.

Lately the churchyard was tidied up by a team of willing villagers of all ages, armed with suitable (and some unsuitable) implements. They made a good job of cleaning up the undergrowth, shrubs, and unwanted trees and exposing a lovely view over the dale. A happy if damp day, with welcome refreshments in the rectory garage, was had by all.

The village has changed a great deal during the last twenty years but still it is not only a village but a lively community.

Beamish

This former colliery village sprang to fame when it was chosen as the site for the North of England Open Air Museum, home of the history of the North East.

Beamish Hall, now an Adult Education college was once the home of the Shafto and Eden families and lies cheek by jowl with the museum in this ideally located unspoilt valley away from the bustle of modern life.

Bearpark

The name is a corruption of 'Beaurepaire' – meaning beautiful retreat and was once what might be called a holiday home for the monks of Durham, three miles away.

This ancient village has seen more change than most having gone from being part of the Prince Bishop's Hunting park in the middle of the 12th century to a former mining village said to have been the model for the world's longest running radio serial 'The Archers' when their local vicar moved diocese.

The original estate of 100 acres was a gift of Gilbert de la Lay of Witton and later it became part of the 1,300 acres from Witton Gilbert to Neville's Cross and the Benedictines built a manor house and chapel as a summer retreat for the priors of Durham.

When, in 1346 King David of Scotland camped nearby waiting for the Battle of Neville's Cross to commence, he and his army of 30,000 men laid waste to much of the area. Monks from Durham were said to have watched the battle from the safe haven of the tower of Durham Cathedral – King David being captured.

The buildings at Bearpark were completely destroyed during the 17th century Civil War and were left abandoned. Oak from Baxter's Wood at Bearpark (which still exists) went to provide timber during the building of the monk's dormitory in the Cathedral precincts.

Bearpark Colliery, now closed, was first sunk in 1872, the first coals being drawn three years later.

The Parish church was named after St Edmund, the foundation stone being laid in 1877 and consecrated two years later.

Binchester

Binchester's Roman bath house survives today to tell a very important story of the Roman Commandant's residence here when Binchester was a Roman town on Dere Street.

The discovery nearly two centuries ago of this most perfect hypocaust system in the north country was exciting then, and still interests the archaeologists today with the excavation of the whole of the area.

Vinovia, to give it its Roman name lies some 200 yards from Dere street and is in the shadow almost of Auckland Castle, home of the Bishop of Durham, and the town of Bishop Auckland.

This area is of historic importance with the Bishop's residence, with a beautiful chapel beginning life as a Norman manor house.

During the Commonwealth period in the 17th century the building was damaged and after the Restoration in 1660 Bishop Cosin spent much in restoring the building and making the former banquetting hall into the present chapel.

Auckland Castle also has a magnificent 800 acre deer park along the banks of the River Gaunless.

In recent times it was a modern road construction which excited the villagers of Binchester, when television personality Anneka Rice persuaded and cajoled people into being involved in a feat of engineering which built a road in record time bringing brief fame to this tiny community.

Bishopton

A local historian, Peggy Hutchinson, wrote in 1940: 'Bishopton Village is pleasantly situated on an eminence six miles west-north-west from Stockton and seven miles east from Darlington. It forms a triangle with the church in the middle. The cream washed houses are quaint with age and lend themselves to the picturesque stately trees which make the village a leafy bower for three seasons.'

The church is dedicated to St Peter. There has been a church on this site since the latter part of the 13th century evidenced by the fact that there was a vicar of Bishopton as early as 1290. The Rev. T. B. Holgate and his 3 sisters rebuilt the church at their own expense between 1846 and 1847 also contributing the bells, clock and books as well as silver plate for Holy Communion. The Old Vicarage has a lock-up cell in its basement where the vicar in the old days was allowed to lock-up any drunks causing problems in the village until they sobered up.

On St Peter's Day, the 29th June, children dressed in their Sunday best would take to church gifts of flowers, fruit or eggs, which were later taken to Stockton and Thornaby Hospital. Following the service, tea was served on the village green, the iced buns being a particular favourite. Sports were held later in the day both for the children and adults. The village still celebrates St Peter's Day each year, but on a smaller scale with a Sports Day for local children.

The old school was built in 1813 and closed in 1966 when a new primary school was opened serving Bishopton and surrounding villages.

The most historic feature is Castle Hill, a fortification consisting of an artificial conical mound with a truncated summit and surrounded by a double trench which, no doubt, would act as a moat when filled from a nearby beck. Recently, much work has been undertaken in order to maintain the condition of the Hill, damage having most probably been done in the days when the Hill was used as a recreational haunt as many villagers took advantage of its steep, snowy slopes in the winter for sledging.

Bishopton claims an official record of fairies. The Parish Register for 1752–83 speaks of the fairies thus: 'John Wright remembers having seen fairies. They were small and draped in green. They once brought his mother a pound of butter which they kept with them for a long time and later took with them to Cumberland.' The fairies were thought to inhabit the fortifications.

The village used to boast a thriving Cottagers' Flower, Vegetable, Agricultural and Industrial Show which was first held in 1878. It is interesting to study the show schedule for 1886. For example, under Special Prizes: 'By Mr Blakeborough, the best Ham, fed and bred and cured by a cottager whose rent does not exceed £10 per annum in the district: Prize of 5s.'

Traditionally, villagers were employed within the local agricultural community with only a few travelling to Stillington Iron Works. At one period there were seven quarries being worked on the outskirts of the village and there were five pubs in the village to service the workmen.

Today there are just two, the Blue Bell Inn and the Talbot Hotel. One of the quarries on the edge of the village has been flooded and has been developed into a windsurfing centre. The Village Hall, situated behind the church, provides space for many activities including W.I. meetings, whist drives, craft classes, French, yoga, toddler groups, karate and many other social occasions.

In recent years a small number of new properties has enlarged the population of the village, most houses having been built behind the existing, older properties. Today, Bishopton, a conservation village, finds itself a typical commuter settlement.

Bishop Middleham

Bishop Middleham was the chief home of the Bishops of Durham until the end of the 14th century, but only grassy mounds now indicate this.

Nearby lived Robert Surtees of Mainsforth Hall whose education took him to Grammar school in the late 1700s and to Oxford where he gained an MA before reading for the Bar.

To his memory the Surtees Society was founded after his death in 1834.

Boldron

Twelve miles from Scotch Corner, travelling along the A66 to Penrith, you see a right turn to Boldron. Running down into the centre of the village, you find The George & Dragon Inn, which provides bed and breakfast and is also our Post Office and petrol station. The village consists of 30 homes and a few holiday cottages. The older buildings are mostly of sandstone with Teesdale slab roofs. One house has a delightful stone spiral staircase. It was not until 1939 that electricity arrived here, and about 1965 when water was piped to homes and water closets introduced.

Despite our size we have both a chapel and a church, at which we have regular services. The Primitive Methodist Chapel was built in 1867. The church was built in 1887 and is actually a mission house and is not licensed for weddings, but baptisms and wedding blessings can take place. The village hall was built by joint co-operation in 1962. We hold monthly whist drives and of course, the regular meetings of the Women's Institute. In summer we have an enthusiastic quoits team who play on the central pitches. We also have two working farms and a family plant hire firm.

As we look up towards the A66 from the village, we see how the lorries slowly lumber up Gallows Hill, where in former days the local gallows was situated. Nowadays, life is very quiet – Kate Adie used to spend holidays here as a child – she would find it very different from the dangerous locations where she now finds herself.

Bowburn

In 1857 Bowburn as we know it today did not exist. There was a tollgate on the open land next to the present Wheatsheaf public house. This was known as 'Crowtrees Tollgate'. There were three or four houses on the site of the Crown Cinema or what is now a bingo hall. A house, probably the present Post Office and the 'Hare and Hound' public house, replaced later with the 'Hare and Greyhound'. Bowburn House, a large stone built farm house situated among trees across the road from the 'Hare and Greyhound'. This did not change until a colliery was sunk in 1904 which commenced production in 1906. At the same time houses were built for the workers and streets of colliery houses were built with a number of private dwellings. After the Second World War there was a spate of new building and a vast council housing estate was built. Around 1925, a mission church of St John was opened next door to the 'Hare and Greyhound'. The foundations of the present 'Church of Christ the King' were laid in 1961 and the church was dedicated in 1978. Bowburn continues to expand, even though the colliery closed in 1967.

Bowes

Bowes is a village situated in the south west corner of County Durham. Its parish boundaries border Cumbria to the west and North Yorkshire to the south, to which county it belonged before the county boundaries were changed in 1974.

The history of Bowes can be traced back to pre-Roman times. The Roman Fort of 'Lavatrae' was built on four acres of land of which the east, south and west walls are still visible. The Norman castle, church and cemetery now occupy this land. Many Roman artefacts can be seen, one being a huge rectangular stone slab bearing a Roman inscription which was found in 1929. This stone can be seen in the north transept of the church together with a translation in English. Other Roman stones and altar stones can be seen in the church and cemetery, and some relics are in The Bowes Museum.

The present castle was built between 1171 and 1187 to help protect the area from the marauding Scots. The castle suffered many raids from the Scots and by 1341 was reported to be badly in need of repair.

Bowes Grammar School was built in 1674 by William Hutchinson who made provision for the education of the children from the parishes of Bowes & Romaldkirk. The School had a scholarship for Cambridge, and the children were educated to a very high standard. This school is still used for the primary education of the Local children.

This school must not be confused with the notorious Boys Schools of Charles Dickens fame of which there were several when he visited Bowes in 1838. He based his 'Wackford Squeers of Dotheboys Hall' in *Nicholas Nickleby* on William Shaw's Academy where several boys had gone blind. The old school has now been renamed as Dotheboys Hall and the building is to be found at the west end of the village. Following Charles Dickens' visit and his publications the school closed down.

The road over the Stainmore Pass, now the A66, has always been an important route for traders and travellers and also for the different warring armies through the centuries and in A.D. 954 Eric Bloodaxe met his death on Bowes Moor and is supposedly buried there.

On a stormy night in October 1797 at a coaching inn at Spital, west of Bowes, George Alderson and his son were sitting around the fire discussing the good prices they had made at the recent Brough Hill Fair whilst Mrs Alderson and their maid Bella sat spinning when a knock came at the door. The door was opened cautiously by Bella, who, upon seeing a bent frail looking woman, with her cloak pulled over her head asked her in. The traveller refused a meal and a bed saying she would rest by the fire as she wanted to be on her way early next morning. Soon the family went to bed. But Bella was suspicious after noticing the traveller wore horseman's gaiters below her cloak and lay down on the long settle and pretended to sleep. After a while the stranger took from the folds of her garment a brown withered hand and candle which she lit from the fire. Placing the candle in the hand she came over to Bella, waving the hand chanting, 'Let those who rest more deeply sleep, Let those awake their vigil keep'. Placing the candle on the table she then chanted 'O Hand of Glory shed thy light. Direct us to our spoil tonight'. Now moving nimbly she unbolted the door and, giving a long low whistle, stepped outside. Bella, realising this was a man in disguise and that there were other men outside, quickly slammed the door shut and pushed the bolts and chain in place. After trying to wake the Alderson family she returned to the kitchen and threw a bowl of milk over the withered hand and candle. The Alderson family awoke immediately, the son grabbing his shotgun. There was banging on the door and a voice shouted 'Give up the Hand of Glory and we will not harm you'. Young Alderson fired out the window and the gang rode away. The withered hand remained in the possession of the Aldersons for many years afterwards. (It was widely believed that a hand from a hanged man, treated and pickled and a candle made from the fat of a hanged man had magical powers to make people sleep, and the only way to extinguish the flame was to throw liquid over it).

In the early 1800s a lion escaped from Wombwell's Menagerie, whose caravans were standing in the street. The lion was eventually cornered in the lane leading to Gilmonby and the keepers with hot irons and several villagers with Hay Forks kept it at bay until a halter was placed around its neck and it was led back to its cage.

Apart from the 'Ancient Unicorn' and the Working Men's Club which themselves offer social activities, there are various organisations offering recreational opportunities in the village.

Bowes Agricultural Show is held on the second Saturday in September, when trophies for horticulture, home produce, crafts, walking sticks and the Swaledale Sheep Breeders Challenge Trophy are all catered for. Children's riding events and a quoits match are also held on the show day.

Another important event in the village calendar is the annual carnival, usually held in June.

Bowes Women's Institute is a thriving Group which was founded in 1929.

'Pennine Way' is the name adopted by the Ladies' Country Dance Team, started in 1987 to dance at the Celebrations to mark the 800th anniversary of the castle. These ladies are kept busy during the summer, as they are booked to dance at numerous events throughout the dale.

The Drama Group stages a pantomime and another production each year keeping all the budding thespians busy.

There are many recognised footpaths within the parishes of Bowes & Gilmonby offering a variety of countryside and scenery; from the bleak moorland to the wooded walks by the river Greta. Wild flowers are plentiful, and the birdlife is very varied.

Brancepeth

The name Brancepeth originates from the wild boar, or brawn, said to roam the area that forms the Parish of Brancepeth. A farm known as the Brawn's Den lies on the perimeter of the village.

The actual village consisted of the castle, church, and the cottages in which the Estate workers lived. 1963 saw the first signs of development when several individual building plots within the Castle grounds were sold and houses built. Since 1973 three small housing developments more than tripled the population and all the worker's cottages are now owner occupied. But despite the increase in housing there is still no shop or pub in the village. Our Post Office disappeared in 1973 with the death of the postmistress and we were without one until 1981, when the present owner of the Castle opened a Post Office in the Gatehouse, a move much welcomed by the villagers.

The castle's history dates from Saxon times. The earliest known occupants were the Bulmer family and in 1174 it passed to the all-powerful Nevilles who occupied it until the Rising in the North in 1569. At the beginning of the 18th century the castle was purchased by Sir Henry Belasyse and it is believed that the Grey Lady who haunts the Castle is the ghost of his daughter who believed that when Bonnie Bobby Shafto returned from sea he would marry her, only to die of a broken

St Brandon's Church, Brancepeth

heart when he chose to marry another. In 1796 the Estate was sold to William Russell, a very wealthy Sunderland banker, who spent a great deal of money rebuilding and modernising the castle. In 1828 the Estate passed by marriage to Lord Boyne – family name Hamilton-Russell – whose family occupied the castle until 1922.

During the First World War the castle was used as a hospital and then became the headquarters of the Durham Light Infantry. It is interesting to note that the wood through which Stockley Beck flows is all that remains of the Great West Wood which, in 1635, supplied the timber to build the Navy's first three-decker ship – Sovereign of the Seas – and it was in the castle rose garden that Lord Tennyson wrote 'Come into the Garden Maud.'

In 1978 the present owner, Mrs Margaret Dobson, moved into the castle and has encouraged those interested in home industries and crafts to work in the castle.

The first recorded incumbent in St Brandon's Church was 1085 and through the centuries only 37 names appear, which seems a small number over such a long period. Again there are famous names, among them Shafto, Duncombe, Neville and John Cosin (later Bishop of Durham) who left us such a wealth of beautifully carved woodwork. The chancel and transepts were added to the church in the 14th Century by the Neville family in memory of their son whose tomb is within the chancel. We are proud of our beautiful ancient church and have a rota of helpers who clean the church and keep the churchyard tidy.

The Village School closed in 1932 and is now a dwelling house and the children of the village attend schools at Langley Moor, Durham and Wolsingham.

We have an excellent Village Hall due in no small way to the members of the Women's Institute. Brancepeth W.I. was formed in 1919, with Lady Boyne as President and at first meetings were held in the castle or the village School. The Hall was opened in 1924. It is well equipped and in constant use; playgroups, brownies, badminton, snooker etc. with special functions such as the Harvest Supper and the Christmas Concert when it is filled to capacity with all age groups. We have a remarkable wealth of musical talent in the village and at each Christmas Concert new stars emerge.

Brancepeth Golf Course, planned by the late Lord Boyne and opened in 1924, is very popular and considered good enough for national competitions. The attractive Clubhouse was originally the Castle stables.

From 1864 to 1965 Brancepeth was well served by a regular rail service. In the war years when the castle was the depot for the Durham Light Infantry, with the Army Camp where Stockley Grove houses now stand, many young soldiers boarded a train at Brancepeth Station on their way to overseas service. We are still very fortunate to have a half-hourly bus service between Durham and Crook. However, it is our misfortune that the main road runs through the centre of the village and we are once again endeavouring to have a speed restriction placed on the ever increasing volume of traffic.

The village today is far removed from the Estate village as it was when only Estate workers occupied the houses. It has become a village of commuters whose occupations cover almost all the professions. But for all the changes we still function as a village enjoying the peculiarities and eccentricities of village life.

Burnhope

The former mining village perched on the second highest point in north-west Durham (the highest being Pontop Pike where the giant television mast stands) has a place unique in history. Sprawled along a ridge nearly 800 ft up with an unrivalled view towards the Pennines to the west, to the coast line in the east and 8 miles from Durham. It is the only place outside Durham City where the Durham Miners Gala has been held. The reason is explained by the date – 1926 – during the strike when miners were not allowed to march through the streets of the city and instead drew 40,000 miners to this hilltop vantage point with Durham in the distance.

There is no official record of the event, but the crowds poured uphill to the spot where they stood to applaud their leader A. J. Cook. Even that number attending the unofficial gala was some feat when it was shanks' pony for the vast majority attending. On Saturday 9th August 1986 they celebrated the Diamond Jubilee of the occasion in an august company including Arthur Scargill and the Bishop of Durham Dr David Jenkins.

It is said that between 1800 and 1914 the mining industry proliferated with villages springing up around a pit head virtually overnight. The simple rows of cottages had large officials' houses usually at the end of the terrace with the sound of cages being lowered and coal drawn a regular occurrence.

The miners worked long hours hewing coal while their wives toiled as laboriously above ground washing in tiny damp cottages made wetter by trying to dry clothes for the whole family indoors in often little more than a hovel.

The owners of the pit at Burnhope were, in 1873 fined for the unsanitary conditions of the so-called homes of their workforce.

The life of the village revolved around the Co-operative store similar to the one depicted at Beamish Museum which actually stood in the next village of Annfield Plain. No longer were they tied to the local employer with tokens to use instead of money.

The village had a number of shafts which were sunk over a century and a half ago. Names like the Fortune, Cuckoo, Pheasant, and Robin were countryside names but it was also a custom to name a pit after a member of the owner's household like Annie or Ralph.

A contemporary of George Stephenson who was also born at Wylam, William Hedley, crossed the Tyne to help make his fortune in mining. He lived at Burnopside Hall which lies below the village on the Lanchester to Durham road.

Burnhopflatts was the original name of the colliery which later became Ibbotson's Syke – a name later used for open cast mining near the village. A shaft at Jaw Blades was opened in 1868 but survived only four years.

After the infamous Sowerby and Fletcher ownership Col. Ritson bought the mine in 1881, and coal wrought from there for him until 1936 when the pit was sold and sold on two years later to the Bearpark Coal Company.

Children in the village attend the local school until they are old enough to transfer either to Greencroft Comprehensive school, or if they are of the Roman Catholic faith, to St Bede's at Lanchester.

Ironically in the latter part of this century when all the pits in the area are closed, Burnhope has been practically surrounded by open cast mining which has stripped the land bare of the coal that was left when the colliery closed and the old waggon way returned to nature.

Burnopfield

Looking at Burnopfield from Byermoor, on the A692, it appears to be built on a long narrow shelf. The high ground of Hobson slopes down, levels out to take in Burnopfield, and then descends rapidly to the Derwent Valley. On this shelf, never more than 300 yards wide, the village has grown to a considerable size.

Originally, Burnopfield was very small, stretching from Busty Bank and Sheephill, to the Fold and Bryan's Leap, a distance of a quarter of a mile. These four places had then a small cluster of cottages each, and are the oldest parts of the village. The old Lobley Hill Turnpike was the only road through.

In 1960 when an old house in Bryan's Leap was being demolished, a stone lintel above the fire-place, bearing the inscription 'J.H.1669', was found. The initials were traced to a James Harrison who was in the coal trade at that time, and thus we get a clue as to the age of the village. People must have lived there for almost 400 years.

Because of the discovery of coal in north west Durham in the 17th century, the coal trade began. Narrow gauge waggonways were laid from the pit-heads and Burnopfield was found to be an ideal place for the waggonways from the Pontop and Tanfield Moor areas to pass through and then continue down the hill to cross the Derwent, and on to the river Tyne for the coal to be shipped. Thus both Bryan's Leap and Busty Bank became focal points in the waggonway system, and more people settled there. Curiously, we find that there used to be four public houses and a brewery in the Bryan's Leap area, and two public houses and a brewery in Busty Bank, all for the convenience of the drivers of the waggons. Of these public houses only two have survived. In the 1890s, one, the 'Grapes Inn', ironically, became a Methodist Manse and served as such until 1980.

Burnopfield is sprinkled with odd-sounding place names, some already mentioned. Busty Bank, so named because a hilly bankside in the village burst and exposed a seam of coal. This hilly road became known as Bursty Bank and later as Busty Bank. Bryan's Leap, no doubt because of some prodigious leap on foot or horse-back, worthy of record. About 150 years ago, Burnopfield was usually referred to as the 'Leap', or in local dialect, as the 'Loup'. A small area near Busty Bank, is marked on old maps as 'Sparrow Hall', and the story is told of a doctor who lived there in the 1960s, receiving a letter addressed to the 'Squire of Sparrow Hall'. It made his day! Leap Mill Farm, partly hidden in a secluded little valley, with its working water wheel, is fast becoming a tourist attraction. Nearby Friarside, with its 14th century ruined chapel and its stories of buried treasure is worth a visit.

Had you walked across Bryan's Leap in the year 1815, you might have seen the lone figure of a man, standing beside an artist's easel, painting a picture of the Gibside estate a short distance away. This estate is owned by the Queen Mother's family, the Strathmores, and the painter, – none other than Turner, the world famous landscape artist. For many years the painting hung in the Tate Gallery in London.

The oldest house in the village, Burnopfield Hall, built in 1720 by a wealthy coal owning family called Newton, has an interesting story to tell. In the late 1760s, Hannah Newton, daughter and heiress to the family fortune, met and unfortunately married an Irish adventurer, Lieut. Andrew Robinson Stoney, who was stationed in Newcastle. They went to live at Colepike Hall, Lanchester. There, his ill-treatment of her became a local scandal, and within a few years she died. With his hands on her fortune of £20,000, he set off for London where he met the widowed Countess of Strathmore who owned the Gibside estate, near Burnopfield. Stoney eventually tricked her into marriage, and having to adopt her family name of Bowes, became the notorious Stoney Bowes. Her subsequent miserable life with him became one of the biggest scandals of the period.

In 1746, during one of his 'Journeys', John Wesley visited the scantily populated village, and preached in a garden in Sheephill. He made several more visits, with the result that a Methodist Society was formed, and in 1775 the first Chapel was built in Burnopfield. It had an upper room above the stable where the itinerant preachers kept their horses during the services. This room was later used as a school. In 1880 the Chapel was rebuilt on the same site. By this time other two places of worship had been built. In 1870, a second Methodist Chapel, and in 1873, the first Anglican Church was built at the Leazes end of the village.

Coal played a big part in the growth of Burnopfield. Although surrounded by colliery villages: Lintz, Hobson, Friarside and Marley Hill, it never had a deep mine of its own. Gradually over the years, it became a kind of dormitory village, and, with the building of a big Co-operative Society Store in 1889, it also became a shopping centre for the miners and their families from the neighbouring colliery villages. From about 1870 onwards development quickened. New streets of houses were built, and members of the Co-op. Society were encouraged to save and buy their own houses. A village school was built in 1872.

During the latter part of the 20th century, the village has grown out of all recognition from its old waggonway days. Several new Council and private estates have been built and Burnopfield has extended both to the east and the west absorbing more of the adjoining area into its Postal District. Burnopfield is now a very popular residential village and with its magnificent views of the Derwent Valley, as well as being within easy commuting distance of Newcastle, the population has grown rapidly.

For more than 100 years cricket has flourished in the village. It has the honour of producing two Test cricketers; Jim McConnon, who played for Glamorgan and England, and Colin Milburn, the 'Burnopfield

Basher', who played for Northampton and England. Tragically Colin's career was cut short by a car accident. Sadly, he died in 1990, and his funeral was the biggest ever seen in Burnopfield, being attended by cricketers from local to Test level, as well as his many friends.

Looking back at the growth and development of the village, maybe the most dramatic change is in the occupation of the work-force. Since all the local mines closed, the number of miners in Burnopfield can be counted on one hand, and they work in the coastal pits. Industrial estates, factories, offices and shops now provide the work for both men and women.

Cassop

Cassop Vale is a Site of Special Scientific Interest – and a good place around which to stroll.

Pilgrims came this way, spurred on by the sight of Durham Cathedral ahead and probably noting the quarrying which goes on today – and has done it is thought from the 13th century. Once the bed of a shallow lagoon with deserts and sand dunes with rivers of calcium and magnesium salts the vale today is a refuge for plants and animals who have colonised the area. Birds abound from fly catchers to water fowl and wild flowers grow in profusion over what was a colliery site.

Butterflies – and you may spot a common blue or an argus butterfly or maybe a dragon fly in the marshy areas provide the nature lover with enough to pack their notebook. Your walk should end on Beacon Hill not far from St Pauls Church.

Castle Eden

Today, Castle Eden is a commuter village; a scattered rural settlement in the centre of the former coal-mining area of south-eastern Durham. Whitbread's Brewery, Castle Eden Eggs, Castle Eden and Peterlee Golf Club, the Castle Eden Inn and a design studio are all thriving employers. Castle Eden post office and village shop unfortunately closed in 1991.

However, the earliest occupation was possibly about 6000 BC.

Evidence of flint working at that time has been found locally and an ore site was situated near the mouth of Castle Eden Dene.

There is little evidence to suggest an early permanent community but it is possible that a British Chief found sanctuary in Castle Eden Dene after the conquest of the area by the Saxons. 'The Castle Eden Vase', a Rhenish claw beaker dating from the 6th century, was unearthed, together with human remains, in 1775 by workmen in a hedge some hundred yards north of St James' Church. The vase is now in the British Museum. Rowland Burdon's account of the discovery dated 6th November 1775 states, 'The mouth of the vase was applied to the skull of a human figure so near the surface as to leave the bottom of the vase exposed in the gutter of the hedge. The body had been lain horizontally east to west, the head towards the east had been covered with a heap of ordinary field stones. The labourer said that the skull and bones appeared entire, but he was ordered by the clergyman of the place to make no further search. I had the curiosity, however, to open up the ground and found a cavity which might be supposed to contain a body and a quantity of deep-coloured soil which I presumed to be the ashes of the bones mouldered by the admission of the air. The vase was full of earth and when emptied appeared to have a subtle aromatic smell.'

About AD 900, land in east Durham was granted to a man called Adfrid who defended it against the Danish invaders. Some 50 years later the village of South Yoden, now known as Castle Eden, was separated from the land granted to Adfrid.

During the next few centuries the land lying between the present Church and the Dene contained a small village consisting of a fortified manor house, some cottages and, by 1143, a chapel which stood on the site of the present St James' Church. The manor house moat was filled in about 1500 when the village was probably in a state of decay. Buried foundations linked by a buried cobbled path are all that remain of this settlement today.

In 1757, Rowland Burdon bought the ruined 'castle' or manor house and lands at Castle Eden from William Bromley. The land was unenclosed, the chapel a ruin but the new owner set about improving the estate. The chapel was rebuilt in 1764 becoming the church of St James and in 1765 work began on the Burdon's family residence, the Castle.

During the latter part of the 18th century a considerable growth of industry took place in Castle Eden village. Many of the local names which have survived into the 20th century originated at this time. The present area known as the Factory was the site of a sailcloth factory built and opened in 1792. The manufacture of sailcloth and corduroys was begun by Mr Burdon and about 200 boys, girls and men were employed in spinning and weaving. The row of houses still remains and gives some idea of the extensive nature of the enterprise.

The principal owners of the factory were the Salvin family. Unfortunately, just before the French Revolution broke out, they had sold goods to the French Government worth £20 – 30,000. As times were unsettled one of the Salvins, with an unmarried sister, went to Paris to try to recover the debt. It was paid but the Salvins were caught up in the Reign of Terror. They were imprisoned and feared execution every day. However, they were released and made bankrupt. After their return to England the factory was closed and most of the buildings were pulled down by the Burdon family in 1796.

Another small industry in Castle Eden in the late 18th century was rope making and a house called The Ropery still exists. It was an industry which sold goods to the Hartlepool Ship Building Company, just as the factory sold sailcloth, bleached at the Bleachery in the village, to the same company. The Foundry, situated at the crossing of the Sunderland and Stockton turnpike road and the Hartlepool Railway, made steel parts for the ships.

Castle Eden Brewery was set up in 1826 by another famous family, the Nimmos. Together with the Burdons, they were influential in the establishment and prosperity of Castle Eden. The Brewery which they developed from the New Inn, shown on maps as early as 1791, has been a main source of employment in the area.

Throughout the 19th century, Castle Eden developed as a definite settlement. A cattle market was held on land to the south of the Castle Eden Inn. A school was built for the village children and a Police Station and Magistrates Court were established.

However, there have been many changes in the village. After the death of the last Rowland Burdon in 1944, the Castle was purchased by the N.C.B. and more recently by Ewan Cowie. It awaits development. The Police Station and Court House have been demolished; the school has changed into a private house. There is a new purpose-built community hall. New housing has been built and older housing developed into luxury flats.

How will Castle Eden develop in the 21st century? It must be allowed to retain its unique qualities and sensitive planning is required for this.

Settlements must grow, however, and reflect the age in which its people live. Castle Eden owes much to the Burdons and the Nimmos. Who will be its influence in the year 2000?

Castleside

The Parish of Castleside was formed by an Order in Council dated 27th July 1873, and the oldest part of the Parish of which there is any reference is Healeyfield Township. Records exist of Healeyfield from the year 1170. There is ample evidence going back many centuries of lead mines and workings hereabouts. The name Castleside is, however, much more recent and is generally thought to have derived from an early tenant farmer (called Castle) whose land was located on 'Castle's side' of what in those days would have been the region's major road. Castleside is a pleasantly situated village overlooking the beautiful Derwent Valley and lies on the fringe of unspoilt moorland and the North Pennines now designated an Area of Outstanding Natural Beauty. Castleside's older houses are all stone built and the village lies some 2½ miles south west of Consett and one mile south of Allansford on the river Derwent.

Like many small villages a great deal of Castleside's history is associated with its chapels, churches and pubs. As a result of John Wesley's visit to the area in 1772 Watergate Chapel was built in 1806 (at a cost of £250) to be replaced by a much grander building in 1878, but this chapel was unfortunately demolished in the 1960s. The village's remaining Methodist Chapel was opened in 1885 and services are still held there. The Church of England, dedicated to St John the Evangelist is constructed of local stone and is a reproduction of a church in Switzerland. It is a neat structure of Early English style and consists of nave and chancel with a porch at the west end. The church was opened by the Bishop of Durham in 1867. Snow fell heavily that day and his lordship's carriage stuck in a snowdrift. He had to complete his journey back to Auckland Castle seated on a snowplough. The Baptist Chapel of nearby Rowley – formerly called Cold Rowley – was founded in the days of Cromwell and is still in use today. Rowley station was dismantled and re-erected to form part of the North of England Open Air Museum at Beamish.

The village boasts three pubs, the oldest of which is 'The Horse &

Groom' originally called 'Lane Ends Inn'. This was a public house long before Consett or Castleside were thought of. In cattle droving days it was a well known call house with its own blacksmith shop and brewery. The inn was kept by one family for 200 years, the last member of which retired when the war started in 1939.

Over the years Castleside has had its share of 'characters'. One such was Jack Bulman, born into a respectable family in 1847, whose mother died shortly after his birth. His upbringing was left to a hard-hearted stepmother. Eventually she and his father and stepbrothers and sisters emigrated to Canada leaving Jack to fend for himself. He began wandering around the district working for farmers and living rough. He died in the workhouse in 1932. Then there was Thomas Raw – Mosstrooper. On account of his misdeeds he was ex-communicated by the church and could not be buried in hallowed ground. His home had secret doors and passages and he was never caught by the King's Troopers. He was buried on his own land. Many years later the stone over his grave was removed to a farm at Satley and inserted in a wall there where it can be seen to this day. Tommy Thompson was also well known in the village. He was employed in the steel works for 25 years but lost his job during the Depression. He became a hermit, living in a corrugated iron hut in woods at nearby Allansford. He had his coffin made whilst he was still alive and often slept in it during the winter months as it was warmer than his bed! He died in 1934 aged 77 in a home for the aged and infirm.

Castle centenarian, Mrs Hannah Brownlee, celebrated her 100th birthday on November 20th 1954. She came to this area from Seaham Harbour and worked as a farm servant before her marriage in 1880. She had five daughters and two sons. The house they lived in for 42 years – at a weekly rent of 1/6d – was where the present Castleside Club & Institute was started.

Cockerton

Cockerton was a self supporting community where agriculture and good meadow land were plentiful and cattle grazing here gave off good yield. In about 1790 a famous ox was bred in nearby Archdeacon Newton, from local stock and a Scottish Kyloe, giving its name to an inn on The Green called the Newton Kyloe. Now the den of the 8th Darlington

(Cockerton) Scout Group who commenced on 10th April 1915 in charge of Mr J. P. Lishman.

Records dating from 1594 show parishioners of St Cuthbert's Church Darlington living in Cockerton. Tenants of the Bishop of Durham, their cottages clustered round the green. While still paying a yearly rent for their homes to the Bishop they also worked seasonally for him. During the 18th century there was also a linen trade here, men worked in their own homes, their looms giving little space for family life. Later in the 19th century these men were thrown out of work when weaving machines were installed in the Darlington Mills, and as always when this happens, it caused great hardship. The last linen to be woven here was about 100 years ago.

The library opened on 2nd September 1976 has a good variety of reading and listening material and is well used by young and old alike. It is a most unusual shaped building, rather like the facets of a diamond. On this site once stood Cockerton Hall.

It is uncertain when the Hall was built but was the home of two Quaker families in the early 18th century and then passed to William Wrightson in 1795. The Wrightsons improved it to make it a very impressive home. At William Wrightson's death in 1806 the property passed to his daughter Nanny, wife of John Garth, who had been associated with the Bishop of Durham and after he died, she built three almshouses on The Green to provide homes for elderly widows, rent free in her husband's memory.

After this, the house was let to a series of tenants, one of them being the Dodshun family, who opened the Hall as a Boarding School for young ladies. Maria Dodshun invited members of the newly formed Saxhorn Band to give a concert in the grounds to raise money for their instruments. They became the Cockerton Silver Band, now a very fine Silver Band with many trophies. Years later in 1912 they bought the Syntax Inn in Woodland Road, opposite the Hall known then as the Garth but now is the property of Cockerton Silver Band Working Men's Club.

Also in this part of Woodland Road is the Drovers Garage and two houses. Here in the time of 1848, the Drovers Inn was used by cattle drovers travelling through Cockerton.

At the Cockerton Association for the Prosecution of Felons held here, many poor out of work weavers were fined for poaching, their only means of feeding their families. After many landlords and very much later in 1925 the licence was transferred from the Drovers to the recently built Traveller's Rest, at the other side of 'the club'. Then later a licence was granted for a petrol station in front of the old building. The Drovers Garage was built when the old inn was demolished in 1965.

A period Georgian cottage next to the Drovers was opened as an orphanage 1870–1897 by Mrs Mary Pease as a home for 11 girls. These girls were educated at the school on The Green and found good employment afterwards. The present owners have erected a small plaque on the wall, in the memory of Mary Pease and the orphanage.

To carry on along The Green is 'Suzie' hairdressers. This stands where once was the Syntax Inn, one of the oldest buildings in the village until 1921, when it was demolished. An Aladdins Cave of a shop was built in its place, selling everything from elastic to furnishings. The inn had thick walls of cobbles, held together with straw and mud and had a thatched roof, with a large back garden running down to Cocker Beck. By 1860 John Wetherall had become owner and kept a 'good house'. He was a keen gardener with many successes at local shows, earning him the title, 'Pansy King of Cockerton'.

The annual quoit day was held at the back of The Syntax and having the only large room in the village, it was used for meetings, auctions and occasionally for the coroner's enquiries but the most important was the New Years Eve Ball. Ladies being charged one shilling, gentlemen 1/6d.

Bridge Cottage, the house next door is very interesting. Built round a cruck frame, these pairs of struts of oak are embedded in the walls about ground level, rising to form arches and then joined along a ridge pole to make the house frame. The walls are of stone, mud and straw, being two feet thick and covered with roughcast. It belonged to the Harrisons (members of the family still in the village) who had a market garden and laundry. In 1881 the laundry provided work for local women for about 50 years. The Harrison family were also involved with Cockerton Silver Band. Later the house was made into two dwellings.

In 1813 Methodist meetings were held in the village and finally a site was bought on the south side of The Green, where a chapel was built. There were financial difficulties but matters improved and finally on November 9th 1817 the foundation stone of the new Chapel was laid by Mary and Henry Pease of Pierremont. The building is now the centre of busy interesting meetings as well as Sunday School, playgroup, mother & toddler club, and a well attended welfare clinic.

Thomas Pickering Robinson gave a cottage on The Green to the

Anglican Church to be used as a schoolroom in 1824 but by 1825 it was too small and a large rectangular brick building was built with high Gothic windows, looking very like a church.

John Coates Hebden, headmaster in 1896 showed in his logbook how life in the village affected the school. Illness of scarlet fever, whooping cough, measles, mumps and influenza sometimes closed the school. Other days were lost by the children helping with potato and turnip picking, gathering mushrooms and brambles. The Hirings in Darlington and Cockerton Feast in August, a very popular local gathering, were reasons for half day holidays and Sunday School children were allowed a day off for their annual trip to Redcar.

As the school became overcrowded by the children coming in from the new estates around the village, some were transferred to the newly built Alderman Leach school and on February 3rd 1926 a new school was opened in Newton Lane behind St Mary's Church.

Later the necessary buildings were extended to the New School and finally in 1960 the school on The Green was demolished, leaving the Yew Tree in the school house grounds still standing by the path across The Green. The original stone from above the entrance of the school, dating back to 1825 has been placed in the driveway of the present Cockerton School.

On the South West corner of The Green is Westfield House, a residential home for the elderly, built in 1973. This was once Ivy House Farm, owned by Mr Bert Bainbridge. He used to deliver the milk by pony and trap and the warm fresh milk in the evenings was simply delicious. Johnsons, the previous owners moved to the Green and were the first people to have gas lighting installed in their home.

The Fountain on The Green has once been in the grounds of the Duke of Northumberland's home. It was a working fountain at one time but has recently been made into flower beds. It was installed where the village pump used to serve the needs of the villagers.

St Mary's Church was built in 1901 and in November 1992, the congregation commemorated their 90th anniversary with a flower festival.

The Cocker Beck runs through Branksome Park and can be crossed by two winding paths, through attractive avenues of trees on the Staindrop Road. One evening three schoolgirls, after setting a friend across the fields were alarmed to observe what seemed to be a man in a top hat and a flying cloak coming very quickly after them. They ran up the steps by the houses in Fountain View on to the road in Eggleston View and on looking around, they could not see anyone at all, either coming towards them, or going away!

Years later still, a hospital worker, obviously shaken, told her friend that on coming to work by bus along Eggleston View, she was surprised to see children playing in the field so early. Looking again, the lady realised they wore white bonnets, long dresses and white aprons, 'like clothes worn in the olden days'.

Other people in 'White Clothes' are the men who play for Cockerton Cricket Club, founded in 1893. Cricket had long been played on The Green and later in 1895 John Kitching allowed the team to use one of his fields in Newton Lane. The original changing room was a cattle shed but the Fryer Brothers, local joiners and undertakers, built the present pavilion.

Holy Family Presbytery was built on The Hill in 1936 on the site of a small Elizabethan Manor. This was the home of Father McClusky. A well loved man by all sections of the local people, he was always interested in the children of the nearby homes, encouraging them by giving gifts of books and inviting them to visit him. Holy Family School behind the Presbytery had been built in September 1928 by permission given to Canon Rooney but soon was too small and the nuns and teachers were constantly juggling the rooms, either for classrooms or church purposes. The faithful parishioners helping to 'set the Church up' at weekends. Later Father Avery tried to get the building extended but died suddenly before this could be done. Father White who took over the parish felt his first priority was to build a church. A great deal of hard work was put in by the people of the church to raise funds for this and on 21st July 1960 The Church of the Holy Family was opened and blessed by the Bishop of Hexham and Newcastle.

Cornforth

Cornford originally was the place where a ford to the Manor mill crossed the beck which was the property of the Bishop of Durham. The first written records are before 1180 and in 1183 was called Cornefords. The village over the years has altered very little, the village green with houses round each side. The village had no church until 1868 when a church was built close to the village green, before then all baptisms, weddings and funerals took place at Bishop Middleham. The village was an agricultural one until in 1835 a colliery was sunk about a mile south of the village. This resulted in a new village, springing up west of the old one – West Cornforth.

Cotherstone

The village of Cotherstone lies in Upper Teesdale between the open moors and the rivers Balder and Tees. In the Domesday Book it is 'Cudreston' or 'Cudhere's farm'.

From the village structure, it looks as if there were originally two settlements round the greens which were later linked together. An interesting and complex system of back lanes and passages led to the open pastures. These were enclosed in the early 19th century, and some evidence of the stripfield system can still be seen. Cotherstone Moor is a regulated pasture still managed by field reeves. On the moor is the 'Butterstone', so called because during the great plague in the 17th century, butter and other provisions were left there.

Another interesting feature of the village is the Hagg, a natural amphitheatre carved out by glacial action near the two rivers, and now used as a play area and picnic spot. On the hill above the Hagg are a few faint traces of Cotherstone Castle built about 1200 by the Fitzhughs, the Lords of Cotherstone. Some of the neighbouring cottages have fragments of ornate castle masonry built into them.

A little further upstream is the imposing Percy Myre Rock situated in the midst of an old hunting preserve. The farm Doe Park is thought to be an old hunting lodge. Tradition has it that a huntsman leapt to his death from the Rock into the Tees below.

This area has long been associated with the making of Cotherstone cheese which now has a national reputation.

The village is fortunate in having beautiful wooded riverside walks with many wild flowers, some quite rare, and if one is lucky, the occasional glimpse of dipper, kingfisher, badger and deer. The Tees is also quite popular with anglers and latterly canoeists.

Most of the older Cotherstone houses were of course, farmhouses and cottages stone-built in the plain vernacular style in the late 17th and early

18th centuries. The Manor House is probably the oldest still inhabited. In the 19th century, larger, more ornate residences in their own grounds were built by Quaker industrialists and benefactors, such as Francis Gibson and Lingfords. After the coming of the railway in 1868, well built terraces and Victorian and Edwardian villa-type houses made their appearance. These were followed after the Second World War, by Council-built houses and old people's bungalows.

Today, with the adoption of the Village Plan and tight planning restrictions, a policy of conversions and in-filling has come into existence. This has now nearly reached saturation point, and the next development will probably be low-cost houses for buying and letting.

Largely because of the in-filling and lack of access there is little room for private garages or a public car park. Consequently the main street is becoming congested with parked cars and heavy commercial vehicles passing through.

The three surviving places of worship are The Quaker Meeting House, built 1796. George Fox the Founder of the Society of Friends visited Cotherstone in 1653. The Methodist Chapel was built in 1872 after John Wesley preached here. It still has two services each Sunday, very unusual these days. The Anglican Church was built in 1881 as a Chapel of Ease to St Romald's two miles away.

There were several teaching establishments in the village including an

The East Green, Cotherstone

Anglican and a Methodist School. The primary School was built in 1964, and won a Civic Trust Award.

The coming of the railway in 1868 transformed the village. Before then it had been a self-contained rural community with nine shops. It was the start of tourism. Cotherstone was regarded as a health resort, particularly by the people of Sunderland. An old Tourist Guide of 1911 advertises rooms to let with the inducement of a bathroom and a piano. Not only did they come for their holidays but many returned to retire here.

In 1892 a Hall was built by public subscription. In view of the large numbers of Methodists and Quakers in the village, the name Temperance Hall came as no surprise. There are now 22 different organisations many of whom use the same Village Hall. The word 'Temperance' has been dropped.

The Annual Flower and Vegetable Show continues an old tradition. Younger village members organise a popular Fun Weekend which brings all ages together. Hannah Hauxwell, of T.V. fame, who retired to Cotherstone, assists by helping to judge the fancy dress classes. As the village goes into the 1990s some electric cables have been put underground. (Where will the house martins and the swallows gather in the future?) New gas and water mains are being laid, and the Trustees are bringing the 100 year old Village Hall up to date, with facilities for the disabled and a modern kitchen.

Residents appreciate an hourly bus service, two shops, a Post Office, two Public Houses and a Primary School.

The population now numbers about 430. It is a very neighbourly village and we are very fortunate in our younger caring generation.

Coxhoe

The first written records preserved are about 1235 when the spelling was 'Cokeshoui'. The village then consisted of about 10 cottages and lower down near the beck a watermill was constructed. There was very little change until 1742 when a turnpike road was constructed from Stockton to Durham passing through Coxhoe and a toll-gate was erected at the crossroads around which a small hamlet grew up to be known as Blackgate, a name derived from the tollgate. By the middle of the 18th century the old village had fallen into disuse and the population moved to where the modern village now stands. Coal began to be mined extensively by 1841 the population rose from 117 in 1801 to 3904 and the landscape changed from agricultural to industrial.

In 1725 Coxhoe Hall was built, probably on the site of an earlier manor house. (This building was demolished in 1952). Perhaps the most interesting thing to happen at the hall was the birth of Elizabeth Barrett on the 6th March, 1806 who later was to become the wife of Robert Browning the poet.

Perhaps Coxhoe, for a small mining village, was unique in having two railway stations – one at the south and one at the north. In 1835 a line was constructed from Stockton as far as Coxhoe and this not only served as a mineral line but also as a passenger line. In fact people travelled from Durham by coach to travel on this line, as Durham did not then possess a railway. In 1837 a line was constructed from the port at West Hartlepool to Coxhoe and this was at the south end of the village.

There was a pottery at Coxhoe as early as 1769. The pots produced were of a coarse nature, brown earthenware bowls, used in cooking or baking – usually cream glazed on the inside and plain on the outside but sometimes the outside would have a brown glaze. Tobacco clay pipes were manufactured in 1851 at the site of the above. The clay used for making these pipes came from Cornwall as ballast in ships to Stockton. The pipes were sold in local public houses and shops. Sometimes pipes would be given free to customers by the landlords of public houses.

Coxhoe had its own Gas Works which produced gas after heating coal, the gas was collected in a gasometer, then sent round the village by a network of pipes. The streets were lit by gas standards before electricity reached the village. In 1839 Primitive Methodists had formed a Society here in two small cottages in which to worship and they also had a day school. In 1865 a Primitive Methodist Church was built and next to the chapel a day school for 100 scholars in 1870. The first Wesleyan Chapel was built in 1840 and a day school for boys and girls in 1851. The present Chapel was built in 1871 and cost £800 and seated nearly 500. In 1864 on the closure of the Primitive Methodist Chapel the two congregations amalgamated and the Wesleyan Chapel is now the last remaining place of Methodist worship in our village.

In May 1867 work commenced on the church belonging to the Church of England and on May 14th 1868 the church was consecrated by Charles Baring, Bishop of Durham. The building cost £2,300 and could seat 450 people. This church was never completed and lacks a tower with a steeple and an aisle on the north side. In 1966 a new Roman Catholic Church was built at Coxhoe. This replaced one at West Cornforth which was demolished owing to mining subsidence. This church seats 400 people, and with the priest's house cost £60,000. In a commissioner's report of 1840 Coxhoe was reported as having 30 beer shops and public houses.

Craghead

The sprawling village of Craghead isn't famous or well-known, neither picturesque or pretty – it grew from the need for coal. Built on a ridge, Craghead is an ex-mining village 7 miles from Durham City. Originally a hamlet of a few cottages and John's Castle Inn, it was part of Holmside Parish in 1869, becoming an independent parish in 1912.

The arrival of William Hedley of 'Puffing Billy' fame heralded its birth as a mining village with the sinking of the Thomas Pit in 1841. The first miners' homes, built at a cost of £45.00 each were very basic and sanitation primitive.

The Oswald (1878) and Busty (1912) were sunk by William Hedley's sons after whom streets were named. One of these, Oswald Street, is still known locally as 'Duck Pond Row' – given when the street was flooded and ducks made the most of the opportunity!

Below the west side of the ridge, more houses were built around the time of the Boer War. The first, Bloemfontein, gave its name to the area – shorted to 'The Font'.

Voluntary deductions from miners wages were used to build aged miners homes, South Moor Hospital and the golf course.

An Under-Manager of the Oswald Pit, Harry Bell was rather a martinet and inspired this verse:

> 'Some say the Devil's dead
> And buried on Pelton Fell
> Some say he rose again
> And they called him Harry Bell'.

The closure of the Busty mine in 1968 ended coal-mining in Craghead. The Colliery Band was taken over by the Ever-Ready Battery Company and still plays under its new name.

A local hero, Private Michael Heavyside, a stretcher-bearer in the Durham Light Infantry was awarded the Victoria Cross.

One afternoon, 1917 in France, a wounded man was sighted in a shell-hole 40 yards from the enemy lines, desperately signalling with his water-bottle. Braving sniper and machine-gun fire, Private Heavyside crawled 60 yards to the soldier's aid, caring for him until darkness fell and two comrades were able to reach them and assist in the rescue. The wounded man had lain 3 days and 4 nights without water and would certainly have died without this brave, compassionate comrade.

Craghead miner George Graven won a 17 mile Morpeth to Newcastle race and received a Gold Medal.

Today Craghead is a quiet village, employment mostly outside. There are some small businesses in the old Colliery Buildings and a Dressmaking Factory. Our oldest building, 17th Century, John's Castle Inn is still in business. A large recreation area at the Font is the venue for football, cricket, bowls and whippet racing. Gardening and allotments are popular as is Greyhound, Whippet and Pigeon breeding and racing. There are two Working Men's Clubs. The centre of Women's activity is the Village Hall which sees many fayres, cake and coffee mornings, jumble sales. It also houses the Social Services, pensioners and convivial clubs, keep fit classes and hymn singing sessions. The WI meet in the Welfare Pavilion on the first Thursday of each month. Four churches supply spiritual needs, Church of England, Roman Catholic, Methodist and Spiritualist.

There are good local shops and Post Offices. The surrounding area is quite beautiful with many lovely walks through woods and fields. Craghead is very close to Beamish Museum, South Moor Golf Club and within easy reach of Newcastle, Gateshead, Chester-le-Street and Durham City.

Croxdale

Croxdale Colliery was sunk in the early 19th century and was finally closed in approx. 1936. Many of the inhabitants of the Colliery and Croxdale itself were miners but are now employed at the local factories. Croxdale consists of a main street along the old A1 (now A167) with a Methodist Chapel and a school (now turned into a Community Centre).

Sunderland Bridge Village which has 2 farms, is a quiet village just off the main road and looks down to the river Wear. St Bartholomew's Church is the main Protestant place of worship but Roman Catholic faithfuls must travel down to the Croxdale Hall, the home of the Salvin family, for their worship. The old church in the grounds of Croxdale Hall originally belonged to the Church of England but was exchanged for the present site when the colliery was sunk and there were more worshippers. Over a century ago St Bartholomew's was extended to accommodate these. The river Wear is crossed at this point by two road bridges and the railway viaduct which carries the main London railway line.

Before the large viaduct was built and the main A1 road was cut to bypass Ferryhill – the main road went up into Ferryhill hamlet. Here, where there is still a public house called the Coach and Horses – coaches and horses were then the only form of transport available by road. One wintry day, the road was covered with ice and snow, the horses struggled to climb the little old stone bridge over the river Wear, when one of the lead horses slipped and fell, tipping the coach onto its side and the two outriders were thrown from their seats into the river where they unfortunately drowned.

Just before the battle of Neville's Cross the Scottish army was encamped at Bearpark, and the English army was encamped on the ridge of Kirk Merrington.

The armies could see each other and each sent out outriders to bring in cattle to feed the armies. They clashed, of course, the first skirmish was fought on a small triangle of land across the river from Sunderland Bridge. Another skirmish was when English soldiers were looking for cattle and caught some Scottish troops between Thinford and Croxdale and butchered them. To this day that stretch of land is known as Butcher's Race.

Further to the East of Croxdale is the village of Hett. Built round the village green – it harboured 5 farms and one daughter church. But now much of the land has been built on and only 3 farms remain and the church closed. Many of the inhabitants worked in the neighbouring mines and on the farms but now most of them commute to the industries within travelling distance of the village. Hett's most famous modern day son is the dress designer Bruce Oldfield, who, as a Barnardo boy was fostered by the village dressmaker, so learning at an early age all about materials.

Dipton

The Parish of Dipton was formed by an Order in Council dated 12th December, 1883, just over 107 years ago. The Parish consists of the village of Dipton, part of Flint Hill, and the farmsteads of Annfield House, Boundary House, High and Low Ewehurst, Fondly Set, Pontop Hall, Pontop Pike, Springfield, High Stables, Stob House, Upper Lintz, Weed Park and the hamlet of East Castle. One must remember that this is the Ecclesiastical Parish and has only a passing relationship to the civil parish or urban structure. It was formed from the ancient Township of Collierley sometimes called Collierley and Pontop which were two freehold manors in the area round the summit of Pontop Pike. Population in 1801 was 539 and in 1901 it was 5224 with 955 inhabited houses and 961 families.

On 1st October, 1896, Dipton was absorbed together with Greencroft, Within and Kyo into the Urban District of Annfield Plain. This is really the beginnings of the political structure as distinct from the ecclesiastical structure. At that time land in the area was owned as follows:

Low Collierley, Stob House, Pontop Pike by Lord Ninian Stuart.
Pontop Hall Estate consisting of two farms by Colonel Thomas Anthony Swinburne.
Loud Farm by Michael Hobson.
Ewehurst, or Smethystrother as it was formerly known, by Miss Surtees and Hon. Mrs Vereker.
Springfield by Mrs Turnbull.

No doubt one can find these names on the deeds of property now owned in Dipton.

The Houses in the village were irregular in disposition and the village has always been considered more picturesque than the villages which were associated with coal mining and had long rows of colliery houses.

St John's Church's foundation stone was laid in 1885 and it was consecrated by the Bishop of Durham on 21st July, 1886. The cost of the erection was £3,400. The first vicar of the newly created parish was the Rev Richard Tuson who had conducted services in the Board School from 1883 until the church was built.

Methodism was introduced into Colliery Dykes or Dipton in 1753 by Robert Fairlamb, a farmer, whose early life was in Ryton. First services were held in the house of one by the Name of Edward Jackson of Low

Collierley Farm, in 1758. Robert Fairlamb lived at Hare Law Farm. The first chapel was erected in 1792, so that for many years services must have been held in other buildings or houses. In 1860 the chapel became too small and it was demolished and a new chapel erected on the site. In 1870 this too had become too small and efforts were made to procure another site. This was not done until 1876 when the new building was erected in Front Street, Dipton. The cost of erection including the site was £2,200. The Chapel was restored in 1894 at a further cost of £400. Seating accommodation was for 400 persons.

Primitive Methodism was first introduced into the County of Durham in 1821. Services first took place either in the open air at camp meetings on the common or in a barn, in 1823. Services continued in members' houses until 1834 when a chapel generally known as the 'Ranters' Chapel', a stone structure costing about £60 and holding about 80 persons was built. This chapel continued for about 39 years when it was sold and converted into cottages and a butcher's shop. This chapel in turn was sold and a new one erected in 1873 at a cost of £920 – chiefly through the labours of Ralph Shields. In 1906 a larger church, school and classrooms was built at a cost of £2,400 and opened on 27th February, 1907. Mr J. W. Taylor, MP and his brother James also a JP were the ablest of workers for this building.

The United Methodist Free Church was built in Front Street in 1876 at a cost of £1,300 to seat 280 persons.

Pontop Hall had the first Roman Catholic mission where Roman Catholics attended Mass from 1748 to 1802 when the mission to Brooms was formed. About this time in the 1790s the French Revolution saw many priests flee from France and they stayed at Pontop Hall, later moving to Crookhall and finally to Ushaw College in 1808. The Swinburne family had their own chaplain – Thomas Leckonby who died at the Hall in 1778. The first church in the immediate area was St Patrick's built in 1929. Roman Catholics of the Annfield Plain, Greencroft, Catchgate Hare Law, Dipton and surrounding areas went to the Brooms Church and Schools up to this time.

Under the Education Act, 1870, School Boards were constituted – in the case of Dipton it consisted of five members. Education was carried on in a wooden building until the completion of the erection of the Board Schools in 1878. The building was planned to hold 750 children and there was also a house for the Head Master. The school had Boys, Girls and Infants Departments and the cost of erection was £7,000. In 1894 there was an average attendance of 500 pupils.

St Patrick's School was erected in 1907 to cater for 320 pupils in mixed and infant departments. The cost of erection was £4,000 on land bought from Lord Ninian Stuart at Bradley Lodge.

Gas services and street lamps came about by the formation of the Dipton Gas Co. in 1872. The capital of the company was £2,000 in £5 shares. There were two gasometers supplying gas to Dipton, Tantobie and White-le-Head. There were 70 gas lamps on the streets of these three localities.

With the advent of the Industrial Revolution and the growth of coal-mining many deaths are recorded in the industry. Just a sample:

1802. December 19th – Accidentally killed by a wagon at Collierley.
Matthew Anderson, pitman, buried at Lanchester.
1856. November 17th. Killed in South Derwent Pit, aged 11 years.
George Brown, Driver of Annfield Plain.
1857. October 14th. Killed in South Derwent Pit, aged 18 years.
Jonathan Graham, Hewer, Annfield Plain.

Burials took place at Collierley (St Thomas) Church after it was opened in 1840 and the parish of Collierley established in 1842.

Later the first cemetery at Hare Law was consecrated in 1891.

With the building of the church there developed many activities such as croquet, tennis and cricket. In the case of the latter there were two teams – a senior and a junior. They played on a field near Stob House against teams from neighbouring parishes. A hockey and a football team were formed. Church and chapel choirs were formed and in the winter evenings there were musical concerts. Bazaars were held and money raised for various purposes. As well as choirs other organisations came about. The Women's Institute was formed in 1933 and flourished for many years. Due to closure of the mines and movements of population, membership dwindled to the point that in 1990 it ceased holding meetings.

Easington

Easington, an ancient rural village, one of a strip of pre-Norman settlements in Durham on the north-east coast linked by the Salters Way.

The village gives its name to the Ward and Deanery which stretched from the Wear to Hart.

The ancient parish consisted of Easington, Hawthorn, Haswell and Shotton.

Bishop Cutheard granted these lands to Britulfine in AD 900–15, then in the Boldon Book 1183 we have a description of village life and the payments made to the Bishop by his tenants. In the 14th century Easington was devastated by Scottish raids, when Robert the Bruce tried to regain his lands. The Black Death struck in 1349 and the ravages of the plague reduced the population of Durham by a third.

We are repeatedly told of the poverty of the villagers and the Hatfield survey of 1382 tells how the havoc wrought reduced the rents to property and lands rather than let them lie wasted. Villagers lived a life ruled by the Bishop, who was Lord of the Manor, their land and homes were held by paying rent with services or crops and helping with haymaking, harvesting and other seasonal work.

They grazed their animals on common land and cultivated their crops in their own strip of land in huge communal fields. Administration was transacted at the Halmote Court, all sorts of minor crimes, land decisions and property transactions were decided here.

The Enclosure Decree Award tells how between 1656–1665 the moors of the parish were enclosed and divided between tenants. There was a religious building here in Saxon times, the 12th century church of St Mary the Virgin stands in a prominent position overlooking a large village green and is a landmark for sailors on navigation charts.

In 1256 it was decreed the perpetual Union of the Rectory and the Archdeaconry of Durham which lasted from 1256–1832. During that time there were many important Rectors, amongst them were Anthony Bek, Robert de Geneva and Bernard Gilpin. The earliest part of the church is the lower part of the tower and the font steps.

The church register which dates back to 1571 is one of the oldest in the Diocese.

In the register is the 'Solemn League and Covenant' upholding the Protestant religion and opposing Popery, it contains the names of 157 male parishioners who in 1654 signed or made their mark, very few copies of these covenants remain in the country today.

Inside the church are two medieval effigies of a lady and a knight in armour, said to be of the Fitz-Marmaduke family of Horden Hall. C1300–18.

Over the centuries the church has been considerably altered and has various stages of architecture, the last major change was in 1894.

Opposite the church is Seaton Holme, once the Rectory, the residence of the Archdeacons.

This is an important Grade 1 listed domestic building, archaeological works have shown signs of a medieval great hall with a cross wing service range.

After the Rector moved to a more modern home, the Rectory became a Children's Home, then an Old Men's Hostel until the residents moved into a new purpose-built Home built in the garden.

The building fell into decay after many years use as a community building by Social Services and local groups. In 1990 the Parish Council bought the Rectory, and after renovation is used for offices and community facilities. The Village Green was used for both pleasure and punishment, in 1569 two men were executed there after supporting the Rebellion of the North in the region of Elizabeth I. Agricultural shows, feasts and fairs were held there and residents living around the Green could graze their animals there.

In the south-east corner is the Pinfold, where stray animals would be kept until their owners claimed them.

The Turnpike road crossed the Green and the Kings Head was a coaching inn. The Royal Mail called daily to collect post. The coaches 'Pilot' and 'Expedition' travelled from High Street, Sunderland picking up passengers on the way south. The Parish Vestry dealt with the poor, then in 1837 a Board of Guardians for the poor of surrounding parishes was set up with Rowland Burdon, Esquire of Castle Eden as Chairman and the Rector, the Reverend Henry G. Liddell as Vice Chairman.

In 1850 at a cost of £2,300 the Union Workhouse was erected with John Mason as Master and his wife Mary as Matron. The number of inmates increased as more mines opened in the district and the population grew, a hospital was built and the workhouse enlarged.

In 1930 the County Council took over and it became Leeholme Hospital, serving the community until the early 1970s, when it was pulled down.

Easington had its first school in 1818, when the Rector, Archdeacon Prosser gave £1,000 to support the school.

In 1855 a new school was built nearby, the school log book describes the problems the Master had with local incumbents and the pupils.

In the 1851 census Easington was a thriving village, the centre of the area with many businesses such as boot and shoemakers, butchers, drapers and grocers. There were four inns and it was surrounded by many farms.

There were five corn mills and another one in Little Thorpe, the Mill of Esinton was mentioned in the Boldon Book.

Jacksons Mill eventually became an Isolation Hospital which closed when a new hospital was built at Little Thorpe.

As the collieries were sunk and the miners arrived from all over Britain, they needed their own churches, the old parish of Easington shrunk and was not such a rich living.

After 1832 the Rectors were not Archdeacons, other religions were starting, Methodism came to the village in 1855 and the present chapel built in 1885. Roman Catholics could worship freely and the Church of our Lady of Victories and St Thomas was opened in 1875 in Clappersgate.

Easington has had its myths, of grey ladies, secret tunnels from the church to Horden Hall. Lewis Carroll is said to have been a visitor to the Rectory, basing Alice on the Rector's daughter, but this is also claimed in other places. There is the legend of the Easington Hare, of a witch who lived on the Green and led the hunt a merry dance by changing from human to hare.

When the coal field eventually reached the coast, Easington Colliery was built and in 1910 the first coal drawn, the shopping area moved there, where rows of colliery houses were built. May 1951 saw a major tragedy in the lives of the mining community when 51 miners and two rescue workers perished in the still keenly felt Easington Pit Disaster. Peterlee new town was planned and that now is more the main shopping area.

East & West Newbiggin

The Parish of East and West Newbiggin, borders on Bishopton Parish and is incorporated into it. It is a very small parish consisting of four farms, and five dwelling houses.

In 1686 Thomas Barker a Country Yeoman or Farmer, paid for East Newbiggin Farm £1.00 yearly to the Parish of Darlington, as part of the Christmas distributions to the Poor of the town. A sum of £5.00 was distributed among the other local parishes by the same Thomas Barker, for the poor, which would have been a large sum of money at that time.

In the 1800s, when Darlington was a flourishing linen town, flax and cotton would be laid out to dry on the hillside at East Newbiggin. Then it was taken to the mills in Darlington and sent all over the world.

In 1829 a farmer from Longnewton, a Mr Harbottle was fined the sum of one penny for leading a pony loaded with corn or flour, over East Newbiggin land; at that time farmed by a farmer Mr Smurthwaite but owned by Watson Alcock Engineering of Stockton on Tees.

The Parish was at one time part of the Londonderry Estate but was sold off to pay Lord Londonderry's death duties on November 15th 1917.

Manor Farm at Little Stainton, between Darlington & Sedgefield, is as pleasant a place as ever saw a murder.

In 1798 a servant girl put arsenic into flour with the intention of poisoning her master, a Mr Atkinson, who it is said had 'taken very great liberties with her.' In the event the mother of the household made bread with the flour and all the family except Mr Atkinson were taken ill.

But only his mother succumbed.

The girl was banished but as she was an orphan and friendless she eventually came back to the farm and was arrested and charged. The girl Mary Nicholson was hanged at Durham but only at the second attempt after the first rope broke. This was thought to be the last hanging on Framwellgate Moor.

Ebchester

The tramp of Roman footsteps from York to Scotland took Agricola's troops directly across what is modern Ebchester on the banks of the river Derwent, the dividing line between Durham and Northumberland.

Centuries later a small museum commemorating the four acre square built fort of Vindomara remains to mark their presence. The village church dedicated to St Ebba was built in Norman times largely using the stones left by the Romans. Buried in the churchyard are members of the Surtees family of Hamsterley Hall, local landowners – including the creator of 'Jorrocks', sporting journalist Robert Smith Surtees, brought to the Hall as a four year old and who lived there for half a century.

Further down the valley lies Derwentcote and an early steel furnace recently restored.

Land owned by the local authority and the National Trust ensures the tranquillity of this lovely area along the river banks.

Edmundbyers

The village of Edmundbyers is known to date back to Saxon times but man has inhabited the area for many thousands of years.

The name most probably originated from a Saxon named Edmund but legend has it that it was in fact named after King Edmund, King of Northumbria in AD 946. 'Edmondbires' is mentioned in the Boldon Book in 1183 in the survey recording the See of Durham, as being held by one Alan Bruntoft, for his service in the Forest.

The village continued in its quiet course for many centuries until the middle of the 17th century when a great change occurred in the religious attitudes of that time. Prior to this time many people in need of medical help would consult a 'wise woman' or 'charmer' in the hope of having ailments cured. From about 1630 an hysterical outcry against witchcraft crept over the countryside and continued for many years, many forms of folk medicine, spells and sorcery being frowned upon.

Edmundbyers was no exception and became famous for its witches and even the Devil himself is reported to have visited the village. One story of witchcraft here is well recorded. During November 1641 Margaret Hooper is said to have become possessed, showing signs of derangement following a visit to a farm at Hunstanworth. She was unable to say the Lord's Prayer and began to foam at the mouth. Mrs Hooper claimed to see a black beast, which struck her feet and dragged her onto the floor before throwing her into the hall. Those present smelled a terrible stench and flames and smoke issued from this monster. As the household knelt to pray invoking the Almighty to save Mrs Hooper, a divine presence like a child with a shining face was seen, after which Mrs Hooper began to recover.

At Newcastle Assizes on April 3rd 1673, records show Ann Armstrong of Edmundbyers attended a witch's meeting and named several people including Mary Hunter of Birkenside, Dorothy Green, John and Ann Whitfield of Edmundbyers with many others, in a famous witchcraft trial. Accusations were made of horses and oxen being bewitched and Mary Hunter is said to have changed her shape to a swallow, flying under and around a neighbour's horse and causing it to die within a week. No record of the outcome of the trial has been found. Most of the so called witches were probably lonely old ladies, eccentric recluses who kept a pet and who perhaps used herbal remedies to treat sufferers. If sickness occurred in the family, or horses or cattle became ill, if crops were blighted and butter would not churn, all were blamed on witchcraft or sorcery.

Many local women and men in the Derwent Valley faced the courts and were proven guilty. Sinister tales of witches who on dark stormy nights flew upon their broomsticks to meeting places and cast many great spells and even danced with the Devil were told at these times. Jane Frizzle was another notorious witch who lived in nearby Crooked Oak. From the antiquated farmhouse with its ornamental doorway dated 1684 on the lintel, Jane is said to have travelled by broomstick, casting evil spells on men, maidens and cattle. Little is known of her or when she died, but some say she lies buried in a lonely field at Greenhead, near Carterway Heads. In those days the wise traveller in these parts always gripped the thumb in the palm of the hand or carried a crooked silver sixpence to safeguard them against evil.

St Edmund's Church, at the west of the village, was founded about 1150 and has an 'eye' window, said to ward off evil spirits. In spring the smell of wild garlic fills the air in the churchyard (a sure protection against witches) and a headstone on the west wall is in memory of Elizabeth Lee who died in 1792, reputedly the last witch to live in Edmundbyers. Rowan trees are planted in gardens of many farmhouses and horseshoes nailed to stable doors to prevent witches from gaining entry or stealing horses at night, and these can be seen to this day.

Eggleston

Eggleston is a lovely village on the north bank of the Tees, seven miles to the west of Barnard Castle. Many of the houses and cottages date back to the 18th century but the village itself is still growing as people choose to live in the quiet of the dale, though must work elsewhere. Eggleston has a long history of settlement going back to prehistoric times, as the

'Standing Stones' at Foggerthwaite just above the village, testify – though most of the circle was dismantled in the early 19th century when the fells were enclosed for sheep farming. Terracing on many of the lower slopes dates back to the ridge and furrow farming methods of the Middle Ages, but the terraced houses were built by the Society of Friends, later incorporated as the London Lead Company, who first came to Eggleston under the reign of William and Mary – perhaps initially to work the mine confiscated in 1571 from the Earl of Westmorland for high treason. Forty men were employed as miners until 1904 when the company closed the smelt mills.

In the early part of the 20th century Eggleston was virtually self sufficient with its own forge, a joiner and wheelwright, dressmakers, shoemakers, even a mineral water factory. All of this commercial activity has now vanished and only the shop and post office remain, but the continued overriding importance of farming is reflected in the Eggleston Agricultural Show, which has been held on the third Saturday of September for the past 116 years, providing a yearly opportunity for countrymen and their wives to compete in all manner of rural occupations as well as the important livestock judging.

Eggleston Hall just north of the medieval bridge over the Tees on the road to Romaldkirk, has extensive and beautiful gardens which are open to the public.

Etherley

Etherley is approximately three miles from Bishop Auckland and twelve miles from Darlington. It was part of the once vast area of the Durham Coalfield which provided work for local miners, for miners at Raley Fell, Gauges Arms, Brusselton, West Tees, Gordon House. The growing demand for coal in the 19th century, brought increased prosperity, and the need for housing and amenities for an expanding population. Also there was an extension of the Stockton and Darlington railway known as the Etherley Incline to Witton Park Station. The name of Colonel Stobart was connected with these mines. The Colliery Office near the Dog and Gun is now private dwellings. The Literary Institute was the venue for social activities and is now known as the Franklin Scout Hall which overlooks the cricket field.

The Church of St Cuthbert, Etherley

The Infant School, next to it, was built in 1901 and closed in 1965. It is now a private house. The Church School built by Colonel Stobart was closed in 1915 when the new council school was opened.

Houses known as 'The Fields' and 'Red House' were used during the wars for war wounded. Red House was demolished and replaced by a council house estate of the same name. Other estates since the Second World War are Bankwell Drive, Rudland Way, St Cuthbert's Avenue, Church View, Witton Way, Garth Meadows and Auckland View and a small engineering factory provides local employment.

The 1926 General Strike led to the closure of many mines and widespread unemployment, until the outbreak of the Second World War. Reverend Lewis Evans found work for some, converting the old school for use as a Church Hall in 1929. In spite of the hardship, crime was almost unknown, villagers action never went unnoticed.

During these hard times women worked as domestics or took in washing. Spring saw them picking stones in fields, in Summer stacking hay and potato picking in Autumn. Men also sought extra money catching song birds to be sold and money to be won playing pitch and toss, if one could dodge the village policeman. Children would pick wild fruits and sell them door to door, beg empty jars to trade for a penny or a gas mantle or admission to the 'Cosy' cinema at Witton Park.

A knuckle knock on a room wall meant that one was wanted next door. A thud of a poker on the fire back warned the rentman was about.

Popping next door was for a number of reasons – to borrow or lend, seek or give advice, encourage or caution, often to help tend illness.

It was a time of amateur healing. Kindly neighbours would offer beef tea to warm you up, or fever cures to cool you down, vinegar cloths for the brow, sulphur for the throat, camphorated oil for the chest, socks full of heated salt on necks, onion poultices and spiders webs and fussball spores on any part they fancied. For an involuntary twitch, what better than a piece of raw meat.

Before the increase of heavy traffic, children played inexpensive games of controlling a large iron hoop with a metal hook called booling, spinning a top by lashing with string on a stick, skipping and handball on the Ball Alley where the engineering factory is situated. There were seasonal games – jarping of hard boiled eggs in search of the hardest shell, conkers in autumn, itchy bay (never called hop scotch), chucks, or What time is it Mr Wolf.

Evenwood & Barony

Evenwood was one of the places given by King Canute to the Bishop of Durham in AD 1000, on his pilgrimage to the shrine of St Cuthbert. The place name was then Efenwoda, an old Danish name for Wild Boar Wood.

In the early 12th century the Bishop of that time enclosed a vast tract of land to use as a hunting park. A section of this wall is known in the village as Stones End.

Evenwood is situated on the south bank of the river Gaunless which flows via West Auckland, South Church, through the grounds of Auckland Castle (home of the Bishop of Durham) and then joins the river Wear.

Not much is known of the Barony which takes in the hamlets of Lands, Morley and Ramshaw, also including part of Toft Hill and West Auckland. It is thought that like the 'Elvet' of Durham it was part of the Prior's estate, the Prior being the chief clergyman of the Cathedral.

At one time a castle stood on the site of the Church Farm where part of the moat can still be seen. The troops of Oliver Cromwell are reputed to have built a hill on which to stand a cannon to bombard the castle. During recent years the Parish Council had the mound of earth put back into the pond and landscaped the ground.

As long ago as 1368 Evenwood was identified with the iron trade when a bloomery was operated, the wood for the furnaces coming from the Crag Wood which consisted mainly of oak trees. Perhaps this was the 'even wood' when viewed from a distance.

Coal was discovered here around 1384. Scottish traders brought their goods for sale or barter and loaded their pack horses with coal on the return journey. Later on when the seams of coal were traced they provided fortunes for the land owners and work for hundreds of people. Families came from as far as Kent, Wales, Scotland, the lead mines in Cumbria, Teesdale and Weardale. By the end of the 19th century it was a thriving place. Railways had also been built around this time, bringing more work and more people.

Streets of houses were erected along with chapels, a church, shops and public houses. The Randolph Colliery, as the mine was named, and the adjoining Cokeworks provided work for all. The men worked hard and drank hard. To combat this various temperance societies were formed and leisure activities were numerous.

The church of St Paul was built in 1866, burned down in 1907 and rebuilt in 1909. Previous to this the village was in the parish of St Helen Auckland, a distance of over two miles away.

A National school was built in 1865 and an Infants school in 1886. The premises are now used as a Community Centre, a modern school being built on the outskirts of the village.

In 1912 Wade Emmerson of Brookside House started a bus service to Bishop Auckland. This is now known as O.K. Travel, with a network of bus routes in south west Durham.

After the First World War strikes and a slump in the coal trade resulted in families moving away, many going overseas.

Trade picked up again during the Second World War and the District Council added four new housing estates to the village; just recently private houses have been put up.

Sadly the mine closed in 1962 and the Cokeworks likewise in 1984. New industries have taken their place and other opportunities for employment are in the towns round about.

A pleasant medium sized village with lots of green open spaces. It has a frequent bus service to Bishop Auckland which is five miles away and also through services to Barnard Castle, Darlington and Newcastle.

Cockfield for bonnie lasses
Staindrop for pride
Evenwood for honest folk
But nearly all have died.

Ferryhill

Ferryhill is a large village situated some six miles south of Durham City, bordered on the east by the London to Edinburgh railway, and on the west by the A167 road, formerly known as the Great North Road.

Several theories exist as to how Ferryhill got its name. One legend states that there was a river, now extinct, flowing through the limestone gap, where the railway line runs, and the ford at the bottom of the hill, combined with the village on the top, account for its name. The second and most popular theory is that in the 13th Century, Sir Roger De Ferry (or Ferie), killed the last wild boar near Cleves Cross – certainly the seal of Sir Roger De Ferie still exists and shows a Boar passant.

Before the Reformation, Ferryhill was the property of the Priory of Durham, and became a thriving agricultural community. Little changed after the Reformation except that the land transferred to the Dean and Chapter of the Cathedral.

During the Civil War, families suffered persecution as supporters of the Royalist or Parliamentary Sides, and one prominent Royalist land-owner was arrested and his estate seized.

In 1599, the plague reached Ferryhill, and 26 people died, but the Village water supply was pure enough to ensure no further outbreaks in neighbouring villages.

The Manor House, which stands on top of the Hill, has stood there since the 16th Century and is one of the gems of the Village. Like all old houses it has had a chequered career, having been a feudal manor, doctor's residence and surgery, orphanage. It is currently a Residential Hotel.

Standing on the outskirts of the village, is the ruin of an old mill, and it was here in 1683 that Andrew Mills murdered the three children of his employer John Brass. He was executed and his body hung in chains at the crossroads to the north of the village.

Little changed in this Village, known for its two village ponds, until the coming of the Industrial Revolution, when a railway was constructed in 1840, followed by a blast furnace in the 1850s.

Coal mining has been carried out in the form of Bell Pits in the 14th and 15th centuries, but in 1902 a shaft was sunk in land north west of the village, and Dean & Chapter Colliery became the main employer of the local inhabitants. Hundreds of men from all over the British Isles came seeking work. When Mainsforth Colliery shaft was sunk in 1904, the population rose again as colliery houses were built to accommodate the ever increasing population. A community spirit, yet a friendly rivalry began between the two mines – there were competitions of all kinds, such as pit pony shows, quoits, first aid, carnivals and brass bands. Over the years, there has been a snowballing of new estates to cope with a growing demand. Schools are plentiful for children of all ages. The elderly are well catered for with bungalows, large nursing homes and rest homes. All religious denominations have suitable premises. Water was once heated on an open coal fire, a 'fireside' boiler, or a 'set-pot' in a back kitchen. For scooping out the water, a lavin tin was used, and a Mr Mann had a thriving business going around soldering the tins at a half-penny a time. Three of the more notable people brought up in the Village are: Jack Scott, a household name as a B.B.C. Weatherman; Charlie Spedding, for his prowess as a long distance runner, and Joe Slater, a local preacher, who rose from the coal face to be an MP, then Assistant Postmaster General and then to the House of Lords.

The Town Hall, built in 1886 with money from public subscriptions, has a garden leading to a large square, where a flourishing long standing open air market is held weekly on a Friday.

A Railway Station, built to accommodate the main London to Edinburgh line, became a victim of the 'Beeching' axe, but there are current rumours that it might well be re-opened.

Outdoor sport such as football, cricket and bowling are well provided for. Also existing are the Leisure Centre and a Community Hall which houses two separate Women's Institutes.

Frosterley

The ancient village of Frosterley in Weardale, between Wolsingham and Stanhope, lies mainly on the north side of the river Wear.

An outstanding feature is the village green edged with a row of lime trees. Originally, a small settlement called Bottlingham, the only remains of this period is a small plot of ground on which stood St Botolph's Chapel.

The main occupations in Frosterley were farming and limestone quarrying. Farming still flourishes as it did in 1183, when it was recorded in the Boldon Book that farmers gave so many days work in the service of the Bishops of Durham. Nowadays farming is mainly hill sheep and beef cattle. The only evidence now of quarrying are the scarred hillsides. The village hall was originally known as the Institute. The money for it was raised by subscriptions of 1d per week, paid out of their wages and built by the men themselves. There is now a good Committee, working hard and fighting to keep it going.

Pillars made from the famous Frosterley marble, unusual for its attractive fossils, can be seen in Durham Cathedral. In 1989 a marble font found in Gainsborough churchyard was restored and installed in the church of St Michael and All Angels, which is set on a slight rise behind the main street.

At one time a street in the village was occupied by Cornish miners and their families who had come north seeking work. The wives taught local ladies lace-making.

On the south side of the river is the Primitive Methodist Chapel and the Junior and Infant School which was originally in the centre of the village. These are linked by a handsome stone bridge built to replace the old one, washed away by floods.

Once there were five public houses in Frosterley; now there are but two. Incomers form a large part of the population and caravanners and tourists abound in what was once a small, quiet village. However, a thriving WI, and various other activities help to make this a very pleasant place in which to live.

Gainford

Gainford is an ancient place, first mentioned by Simon of Durham in 801, but known to have been a monastic establishment long before that. In time it became the centre of a large seignory, which included many small hamlets, such as Langton, Piercebridge and Streatlam. One of these was Alwent, now a farm, but in the 14th century a manor, where lived John, a notorious adulterer. In 1313, he was arraigned before the bishop and confessed to adultery with Agnes of Raby and Annabella of Durham and could not deny that he had committed the same sin with Annabella of Barnard Castle, Christiana Clergis and Emma le Ambelour. John of Alwent must have been a man of means to have visited ladies in places as far apart as Durham and Barnard Castle and a person of consequence, since his sentence, though severe, was not penal. He was to be whipped round the churchyard of Gainford, dressed only in a linen shift, on six successive Sundays and festivals, and likewise round the market place of Darlington on six Mondays, then as now market days, at the time when the streets would be thronged. He was to be publicly admonished; and if he did not fulfil the conditions of the penance, he was to be excommunicated. This was the severest punishment of the law, since it meant that the victim was excluded from the church and local society, and open to indiscriminate attack. A strange coincidence is that 350 years later, when parish baptismal records were first kept, two illegitimate children, recorded on the same page, were said to have been fathered by an Alwent!

John Cradock, who became vicar of Gainford in 1594, was a man of very disparate qualities. A doctor of divinity and builder of Gainford Hall, spiritual chancellor and Vicar General of the diocese of Durham, he was nevertheless the subject of a complaint in the House of Commons in May 1621, and again in May 1624, of extortion and theft. When a parishioner, Allinson, a man of means died, Cradock held the funeral service, and in the course of it, sent two men round to the house, to seize Allinson's money. He had also taken bribes and forged excommunications, for which offences the committee thought that a fine of 5 marks would be reasonable. When he died in 1627, of poison, it was widely suspected that it was his wife, Margaret, the mother of his eight children, who had administered the fatal dose. She was, however, acquitted.

Great Burdon

In the year 1541 Henry VIII bequeathed the village of Great Burdon to the Prior and Covenant of Durham, known today as The Dean and Chapter of Durham. From that date until about the Second World War villagers paid rent to Durham Clergy. In those early days farms were built near together as a protection against highwaymen and vagabonds. The village originally had three Farms, a mill, a blacksmith shop, a pub and several cottages. According to the *London Gazette* dated December 10th 1872, the larger part of Great Burdon was rented to Mr John Feetham, who lived at Toft Hill Farm. Mr Feetham and family were well known in the district and were very often seen riding along the country lanes on a bicycle built for six people. The outside appearance of this farmhouse has not changed through the years. In recent years the name has been changed to Great Burdon Farm.

The farm next door was once thought to have been part of a coaching house. Evidence of this is shown on the walls of some of the buildings. The bricks are formed to make archways, probably to accommodate horses and coaches. There are many stories told about this house. It is supposed to be haunted. A traveller who after partaking of the landlord's potent brew, went upstairs to bed. No one told him about the two steps into the room. He fell down and broke his neck. Since then he has supposed to have haunted that part of the house.

The mill which is called Mill Batts Farm is one of the oldest buildings in the village, dating back to the 12th century. Until the 1920s a mill race diverted the river Skerne to work the mill. This was substituted by a 22 h.p. oil engine by Mr Jones. The miller ground corn for many of the farmers in the district. Some were so poor they could not pay in cash. When this happened the miller took so much ground corn from each bag in payment. The house and mill remain the same today. The interior of the house is still as picturesque as ever with the beautiful old beams in the rooms.

The blacksmith's shop across the green was a going concern until the late 1970s. There was a small house attached to the shop. Before tractors and cars took over, the blacksmith was a very busy man, shoeing horses and repairing farm machinery. Today the front of this building looks the same but the interior has been refurbished and is used as a private dwelling.

The pub which was called the Black Horse was situated at the end of the row of houses facing the green. After the last landlord retired it was turned into a private dwelling. Many tales have been told about the happenings in the pub. One tale is about an old man who got drunk at least twice a week. After closing time he would tumble into his cart and his faithful old steed would take him home. One night some of the young bright sparks in the village thought they would have a bit of fun. When the old man came to the pub they unhitched his horse and passed the shafts through the gate before hitching up again. Closing time came and the old man climbed into his cart and fell asleep as he always did. Imagine his surprise when he woke the next morning to find himself still outside the pub instead of at home!

The farm in the corner of the village green called Cargott Farm has remained the same on the outside although the interior has been modernised. Many years ago a farmer who lived there lost his wife. A few years later he and his son married two sisters. All went well for a few years until the son ran off with the blacksmith's wife, leaving the father to look after the two families. A hard task for a man in those days when Government Aid was unheard of.

The large old House facing the Green was rented for years by the Blair Family, the last family member being Miss Blair. The House has now been sold. Many years ago this house was rented to a Mr & Mrs Wooler who lived for several years in India before coming to Great Burdon. On the 27th of June 1855 Mrs Wooler died. Her remains were placed in a grave in Haughton churchyard, but shortly afterwards disinterred and examined because of a rumour having got about that the unhappy lady had been poisoned. The result of the post-mortem examinations showed the discovery of arsenic. Mr Wooler was subsequently arrested and sent for trial at Durham Assizes. People said he escaped the gallows because the eloquence of Sergeant Wilkins, whose theory was that it was a custom prevalent in India for ladies to take small doses of arsenic for their complexions. Mr Wooler was duly found not guilty of Murder and spent the last sixteen years of his life in Haughton. When he died his remains were placed in the same grave as his late wife.

Old buildings have been pulled down to make way for better roads and new houses, but still Great Burdon has not lost its charm, and remains still a very nice place to live.

Great Lumley

Great Lumley is a village with about 4,500 inhabitants, situated on a hill overlooking the river Wear with beautiful views of the surrounding countryside. It is about three miles from Chester le Street and close to Lumley castle from where the village gets its name. The local landowners for many centuries were the Lumleys, later to be ennobled as Earls of Scarborough.

In 1801 the population was recorded as 696, the majority earning their living in the coal mines or on the land. The present population have to commute to Newcastle, Sunderland, Durham or Washington because the coal mines have closed, there is little local industry and the farms are now highly mechanised.

In 1635 Sir John Duck Bt, endowed a hospital, (or almshouse), for twelve poor widows, with forty pounds per year to be shared amongst them. Duck's Hospital continued to be a home for poor villagers until the early 1950s when it was demolished. The hospital consisted of single roomed houses built around a square in the centre of which was the communal water pump. The oil lit houses were very small and dark, some were fortunate enough to have a view over the river Wear but the majority faced into the square. A curfew was rung every evening and the gate closed. The bell is all that remains and that is kept in the parish church. The money is still distributed annually but now it is used to give parcels to the recently bereaved – either widows or widowers, thus bringing a modern use to an ancient charity. The Henry Smith Charity is also distributed to the needy, who can apply for help, at Christmas.

Over the centuries the village has had its share of tragedy and scandal. One of the most famous tales being the murder of Annie Walker which is recorded in Surtees' *History of Durham.*

In 1632 Annie Walker was living with her uncle and acting as his housekeeper. Rumour had it that she was pregnant and when she disappeared everyone assumed that she had gone away, to where she wouldn't be known, to have the baby. A few months later a miller, who was working late grinding corn, was confronted by a wild eyed apparition dripping blood from five wounds. It was Annie Walker who said that she had been murdered on the instigation of her uncle, the father of the child. The murderer was Mark Sharp, a collier. She had been sent with him, as she thought, to a distant relative to give birth, but he took her to the fell, killed her with a pick used in coal mining and threw her down a nearby mine shaft. He buried the murder weapon and his bloodstained clothes nearby. She told the terror-struck miller that she would continue to haunt him until he informed the authorities of exactly what had happened. This she did until the poor man did as he was told. Upon investigation, everything was as she had said. The uncle and the collier were arrested and subsequently hanged at Durham prison. There have been many other crimes over the centuries but none solved by this unconventional method.

The modern village still has plenty of inhabitants who can trace their ancestors in village history, their names cropping up time and time again in the records but newcomers are always made welcome.

Unfortunately, most of the old village has disappeared and has been replaced by modern houses and bungalows. The village community centre offers a wide range of indoor and outdoor activities, including a fairly successful football team, and the local churches, WI, scout and guide movements are very active in the village. There are a few shops and an excellent doctor's surgery. Children can attend infants and junior school but have to travel to Chester le Street to the local secondary comprehensive school. The original village school built as a national school around 1853, is now used as a snooker club.

All in all, a very good place to live.

Great Stainton

Stanweg-Tun (Saxon), Staninctona (11th century), Stainton in Strata, Stainton in le Street, Stanton le Strete (13th–14th century), Staynton in the Streete (15th–17th century), Great Stainton (17th century), Stainton-le-Street (early 19th century) and back to Great Stainton in 1856.

Great Stainton developed originally to the north of the present village where there are traces of foundations in the neighbouring fields and a place still called Cross Hill is supposed to be the site of a stone cross of a type which were very common in ancient times. It may well be that during the Roman occupation of Britain a small colony or fortification might have existed in the same area as Great Stainton, and although there is no firm evidence of this, coin finds and the name Stainton-le-Street indicate that the village was a key point built on or near a Roman road in the days before Christianity was established. The road ran through the centre of the Parish from north to south leading to Old Durham. Maps dated 1827 use the name of Stainton-le-Street for the village itself but by 1857 it was renamed Great Stainton and by 1923 the Parish also became known as Great Stainton.

The Parish of Great Stainton used to include the townships of Stainton and Elstob and covered nearly 2,000 acres. In 1823, as at present, it consisted of a few houses only, but the 17th century name of Great Stainton would indicate that at that time it was at least of more importance than Little Stainton. Elstob was eventually passed to the Marquess of Londonderry and in 1826 it was bought by the Earl of Eldon.

The church, which is dedicated to All Saints, stands on the west side of the road. There was almost certainly a pre-Conquest church at Great Stainton, probably on the same site as the present building, which is thought to be the third church to be built in exactly this position. The present church was built in 1876 at a cost of £1,767 of which the Earl of Eldon contributed £600, the remainder being by public subscription. Designed by Mr J. P. Pritchett, architect of Darlington, in the Early English style it has a chancel, north vestry, organ chamber, nave, south porch and west tower with spire. Nine fragments of medieval grave covers were built into the north wall of the tower. On the ledge of the west window under the tower there is a piscina bowl (pre-Conquest or thirteenth century), a base of a gable cross and part of a grave cover (probably Saxon or maybe medieval). The bell tower has a single bell with no inscription or date. There is seating for 160 people in the congregation which would indicate a faithful following. The Parish Registers commenced in 1561 and the first recorded Rector of Great Stainton was in 1129. An Order in Council in 1927 combined the previously separate parishes of Bishopton and Great Stainton.

In the 13th century Richard de la Hay who had acquired the manor, obtained special permission to build a mill either within the village or outside of it. By the 16th century the mill had disappeared, and from a survey in the reign of Elizabeth I there was nothing to indicate that it was ever re-built.

In 1719 Mary Baker gave £5 per annum from the rent of the village garden to the poor of Great Stainton and for many years this was put into the Darlington Savings Bank, in the name of the Rector, and the interest given to poor females. The Mary Baker Trust is still in use today (though not just for poor females).

A school was founded in 1749 and was kept by Thomas Ingemethorpe who had formerly been headmaster of Durham. The Rector, Rev Thomas Nicholson, granted £100 and land for the maintenance of a schoolmaster in 1745. In 1847 a National School with teacher's residence was erected by subscription at a cost of £245 and at that time 12 children attended the school. The school is now the village hall and the teacher's residence is in private ownership.

From the Ordnance Survey map of 1856 the Kings Arms public house is shown as well as a Smithy located south west of the village green on the main road, with a letterbox fixed to the west wall. There were also five dwelling houses on the south east side of Cross Hill, the remains of one being used today as a barn. The village pump was enclosed in a cast iron fence to commemorate Queen Victoria's Jubilee in 1877 and is now a Listed Monument.

In 1876 there were 126 inhabitants of Great Stainton Village housed in approximately 18 dwellings, and today there are some 66 residents in 23 dwellings.

Hamsterley & South Bedburn

'Hamsterley Hungertown stands on a Hill'. So goes the old rhyme. Strung along a ridge between the two great river valleys of the Wear and the Tees, the village today belies the fact that records of 1857 show a collection of poor houses, their thatches in ruinous decay. Now with a population of about 600, Holmesterlee, signifying a holme or flat land above a river and lee the hillside above it, is everything a 20th century village dweller could wish for. Still agricultural in the main but with incomers since the Second World War bringing different professions and occupations, a good mixture of young and old means a thriving primary school and an energetic Community Association in the Village Hall. A general store, a butcher's shop and Post Office give excellent service whilst on a higher plane one of the oldest Baptist Meeting Houses in the County, a Methodist Chapel and the Anglican Church of St James provide for our spiritual needs. All a very far cry from the sad picture painted in the old rhyme. In the 'Hungertown' days it was the small settlement of South Bedburn beside the river Bede just below Hamsterley that flourished. Under the Lordship of the Bishops of Durham the copyhold tenures gave the farmers of South Bedburn a security not enjoyed by Hamsterley.

From very early days there was a record of lead mining in the area. A fortified encampment above the Bede suggests a Roman garrison to protect the lead miners, and the mill at South Bedburn was the seat of many enterprises. A cotton mill, stocking factory, sawmill and edge tool manufactory all took their turn and enriched the local families. Now the mill has gone and the hamlet lies at the edge of the extensive Hamsterley Forest. Planted in 1930 and managed by the Forestry Commission, the whole area is extremely beautiful with great stretches of hard and softwoods blending into the high moorlands. People come from all parts of County Durham to enjoy it. The well-known botanist who lives nearby, David Bellamy, has brought the forest and its streams to a wide audience through his television programmes.

Right in the middle of the forest stands The Grove, home at one time to a branch of the Surtees family. R. S. Surtees is remembered for his 'Jorrocks' tales of the hunting field. Recent owners of The Grove tell of meeting the ghost of a Surtees who, riding home after dining too well, fell into the Bede and drowned. If Hamsterley ghosts appear anywhere,

Hamsterley Village

then one can imagine them in the mysterious walled enclosure known as 'The Castles' built on the slopes above the Harthope Burn. There are many archaeological theories about the site and the men who carted the stones to create the massive walls. An account of 1903 suggests that it was built by the Brigantes tribe to protect themselves against the advancing Romans. Edward Wooler then goes on to reason that evidence of lead furnaces nearby could mean that 'The Castles' were used as a penal settlement in which the Romans kept slaves and convicts to work the lead. But so far the stone walls have not given up their secrets.

Extensive greens unite the village houses. 'Beware Ducks' signs warn of the hazard of wandering ducks and geese making for the pond and the motorist is fairly quickly through the village and out onto moorland. The custom of Beating the Bounds was a necessary precaution in days gone by for villagers to protect their common lands. The last Hamsterley and South Bedburn Beating took place in 1977 when a large group walked the Bounds and faithfully observed the tradition of bumping the youngest children on the Currock or boundary stones. Sadly not all the traditions have survived. The Hamsterley Hopping in August must have been a great occasion. Originally these festivals were feasts of dedication to the patron saint of the Parish church, but the religious tenor became submerged and an early writer states that 'climbing up greasy poles, grinning through horse collars, leaping in sacks and other unmentionable feats' formed the staple of amusement. Today we have our Church Fair and the Village Pigeon Shoot. Enjoyable but tamer!

Tamer also seem the occasional acts of vandalism in the village compared with the 19th century records of murders, suicides and thefts. Drunkenness was rife and in 1871 the villagers beheld the Baptist worthy and master blacksmith, John Coulthard, 'drunk, riotous and beating his wife in the middle of the road'. Early in the 1800s the County was riveted by a scandal concerning a Hamsterley landowner. The story of adultery and cruelty involved George Thomas Seaton Blenkinsopp, JP, of Hoppyland Castle and his wife Harriet. After years of abuse and starvation, while her husband made hay with the maid, Jane, Harriet obtained a divorce but her life thereafter seems to have been one long legal battle to obtain her alimony of £160 per year. George now lies in the Parish Church – only seven mourners at his funeral, including his Jane, and encased in three coffins: one of lead, one of oak covered in crimson muslin and one of fur with a mattress and pillow. Harriet survived him by 12 years and no further mention is made of Jane.

'Hamsterley Hoppings, West Auckland Fair will never come back to our mothers nay more' continues that old rhyme. Past, present and future continue to make Hamsterley and South Bedburn, surrounded by some of the loveliest countryside in England, what it is today, a village unique to all of us who live here.

Haswell

Haswell is situated some eight miles east of Durham City and is one of the largest old townships in the Easington Parish. It consists of three parts, Haswell, Haswell Plough and High Haswell. The original village of Haswell was sited at High Haswell where now only a few farms and dwelling houses remain. However, there is a wonderful view from High Haswell of Durham City and the hills behind. The old English name for Haswell was 'Hessewell' meaning hazel well or spring, and today there is a terrace at Haswell Plough called Hessewell. Haswell village and Haswell Plough lie to the south east of High Haswell and are a mixture of private and council houses. There are a number of farms surrounding the village which has a C.E. Church, a new Methodist Chapel, recently opened and a Community Centre where various organisations meet including the WI. There is a primary school and nursery. Part of the original school is occupied by Mencap which does a great deal of good work throughout the region. There is also a residential home for the old. The building was an old manor house brought up-to-date yet still retaining its old characteristics. There are three doctors' surgeries with a chemist shop.

In days gone by Haswell boasted a thriving cattle mart but this has been reduced to a fortnightly auction of various tools, timber, etc. However, at Christmas they still hold a poultry sale. Before the discovery of coal in 1831 the area was totally rural but with the sinking of the shaft the colliery came into being lying between Haswell and Haswell Plough. In 1844 disaster overtook the colliery when a large explosion caused the death of 95 men and boys. After this, because of the lack of provision for the miners' dependants, the Miners' Association started their own welfare scheme. The mine closed in 1895 when the men transferred to nearby collieries. The old colliery houses at Haswell Moor were acquired by the Durham Miners' Association to provide aged miners with houses. There is still part of the old winding house standing as a memorial of the first steel rope winding house in the country.

With the closure of the colliery, Haswell has gone back to being a rural area and most people of working age commute to other parts of the industrial north. However, much has been done to revitalise and up-date the village. A small new estate of privately owned houses has been built on the edge of the village and the Council has demolished derelict old buildings and grassed the areas and planted innumerable trees, shrubs, bulbs etc., and the appearance of the village has improved greatly. After the closure of the railway the Council has made a walkway from the village to Hart (on the coast) stretching nine miles and this is very popular with residents and ramblers from all over the area. The community centre is very modern having recently acquired a bowling green.

Several well known public figures originated from Haswell, namely former MP for Easington (Jack Dormand now Lord Dormand of Easington); Tommy Simpson the well known cyclist who won the Tour de France, Peter McKenzie (the new Methodist Chapel has been named after him).

Although the population has decreased drastically over the past few years especially with the decline of mining, Haswell still remains a quiet close-knit community.

Haughton-le-Skerne

Haughton-le-Skerne was a village until in 1930 the Darlington County Borough extended its boundaries. It is still affectionately referred to as 'The Village'. The name is derived from the 'tun' homestead or village and 'halth' low lying near a river. 'Le-Skerne' after the river which runs close by.

A journey through the village starts by crossing the Skerne bridge, coming out of Darlington. On the right behind some trees stood Red Hall. It was built in 1830 as a residence for Captain Colling. The famous Shorthorn Cattle were originally bred by the Colling Brothers, relatives of Captain Colling. The Hall was bought in 1965, knocked down and most of its 25 acres turned into a Council Housing estate.

The School on the left, was built in 1814, and has passed from school to commercial use. It was originally built with housing for the Schoolmaster and two classrooms. As the village grew the building was extended, but soon it was inadequate and classes had to be held in the Church Hall, and the Village Hall. The School closed in 1973 with the completion of a new school built on Red Hall.

Next is St Andrew's Church which was built c1125, its tower being added some 50 years later.

The first Parson of Haughton is recorded as being Reginald in 1131. In 1861 Mr Cheese, son-in-law and Chaplain of the Bishop of Durham, was appointed Rector. This caused a national outcry, and with a stipend of £1300 a year at stake there was little wonder. It even provoked a cartoon in Punch magazine. Mr Cheese, however, was held in high regard, and during his 25 years saw churches being built at Whessoe and Coatham Mundeville, both in the then Parish of Haughton.

The Church has three bells one of which is of pre-Reformation date, it has part of a reversed alphabet cast on its side. The other two date from 1664. The bells have recently been re-tuned. This was a costly undertaking, with the £14,000 being realised by grants, donations and unstinting generosity both in time and money by the people of Haughton.

An unique event takes place in St Andrew's Church on Advent Sunday. All the Sunday School children receive an Advent Bun, similar to a spiced teacake. It is baked to a secret recipe. At the start only the local baker had the recipe, but now its secret is in the custody of a select band of ladies who bake them. At the outset the custom is thought to have been for the benefit of the poor of the parish.

Butler House, opposite the church was the original rectory and is said to be the oldest domestic building in Darlington, dating back to the 1200s. The present rectory was built c1750 as an extension to Butler House, with a passage joining the two buildings. Now they are separate dwellings, and at the division of the two after the Second World War the original rectory was named after its most illustrious occupant, Bishop Joseph Butler who was Rector from 1721–25. The Church Hall was once stabling for horses & carriages whilst their owners were in church. A stone mounting block is still in situ by Butler House.

There are three churches in Haughton, St Andrew's, Haughton Methodist situated on the Green, and St Ann's R.C. Church, which is in Welbeck Avenue.

They have a good working together relationship and for a number of years they organised a Christmas party for the Senior Citizens of the parish. These eventually outgrew practicality as the register increased, so it was agreed to present each parishioner over 70 years old with a plant. At Christmas 1991 over 600 plants were delivered on the same day, no mean undertaking.

Haughton Green today looks similar to that of 100 years ago. Many houses are listed buildings.

G. A. Fothergill, a well known antiquarian, wrote the following of seven elm trees that graced the village:

Still Proudly gracing Haughton's Green
'The Seven Sisters' stand
No vandal yet hath dared t'outrage
Or harm that beauteous band

Unfortunately that isn't true today, but in their place stand Beech, Lime and Chestnut Trees, many on the green underplanted with bulbs.

The name of William Bewick, the artist is commemorated by a stone in the churchyard, and a door Knocker to this effect on Bewick House, his home on the Green which is near the Highland Laddie Inn. Mr Bewick was famous for his portraits, some of which hang in the National Gallery in London.

Dog Kennel Lane, now known as Kennel Lane on the right side of the Green, was for the dogs from Colonel Trotter's home next to it: Haughton Hall.

Mill Lane, further on the right of the Green as its name suggests, once led to a flourishing mill. John Kendrew had a Flax Spinning Industry there, the very first flax to be spun by machinery. He also discovered a process of grinding glass. Kendrew Street, in Darlington is named after him.

The large building on the right as you leave the village is the Village Hall. This was built in 1926, and under trusteeship was for the Women's Institute. It was in great demand for functions. Farmers Balls, village hops, craft fairs etc. During the 1939/45 war it housed troops, and sometimes was used for schooling. In 1986 it was sold and converted into a nursing home for the elderly.

The last link with Haughton-le-Skerne is with the crossing of the river again into Great Burdon, and on to Stockton.

Helmington Row

Situated between Crook and Willington is the one time colliery village of Helmington Row (originally ELMYDEN RAWE). Although the village still remains, there are no longer any collieries at all in the area, which was once the heart of the Durham coal fields. The colliery closed in 1931 when Pease & Partners sold Bowden Colliery and it became part of the larger mine of Brancepeth and was worked from there. There was a Depression in the area in 1926 when the collieries were closed for 26 weeks, due to great unrest among the miners, and it was about this time the Social Centre was built in the village. The men used to gather there to discuss the troubles in the mines and Union Meetings were held there. They also repaired boots and shoes, made toys and pieces of furniture, there being no money to pay for these things. Another activity in the Depression was hand ball competitions, being held in the colliery villages, the teams being greatly supported by their villages.

The Chapel was the centre of the village life in those days. Everyone gathered together for the Sunday services and even when people moved from the village to the surrounding area they still returned to Chapel on Sunday until it was closed in 1987. Another sign of the times. They also used the Chapel to hold concerts. A well known lady in the village, Miss Reson, produced these concerts for many years, nearly everyone helped, either taking part or making costumes etc. These concerts were greatly enjoyed as no-one could afford to go out of the village for entertainment. The Soup Kitchen for the village was held in the school room of the Chapel and the children were given a daily meal.

In 1948 Helmington Row WI was formed by Miss Nicholls. The first meeting was held in the Chapel school room, but meetings are now held in the new Village Hall.

In 1988 vandals broke into the old Village Hall, the result being it was destroyed by fire. The village was both shocked and angry at this happening to their Hall. In the true village spirit people came together to try to salvage at least part of the Hall. They formed a committee and began to plan a new Hall, holding bingo etc, having raffles. The fire insurance received was £15,000, and DCC gave a grant of £22,000. Wear Valley Council drew up plans for a new building without charge. Councillor Pendlebury and Mr John Richardson gave their help and support. At last they were able to go ahead with the new building. This was completed in 1990 and was opened by Councillors Mrs Lee and Mr Pendlebury.

Until 1963 Helmington Row had its own school, but due to the re-organisation of the education system it was closed, the children now have to travel to Crook and Willington.

The area Isolation Hospital was also part of the village, one ward being used for TB patients. There was a lot of TB at this time due to poor conditions and lack of good food in the Depression. Most of the patients came from the Jarrow area, where there was great poverty. It is now used for the chronically sick.

The people of Helmington Row now have to travel to their work as there is no employment in the village.

Horden

The story of Horden is in many ways the story of all the coastal pit villages, like Blackhall and Seaham. Before the colliery was opened in the late 19th century on land owned by Colonel Burdon of Castle Eden this stretch of coastline was one of wooded denes running down to sand duned beaches, with farming the main occupation of this sparsely populated area.

The prospect of work at the colliery brought miners here mainly from the lowlands of Scotland coalfield but it attracted men from Ireland and skilled workers from as far away as South Africa and Canada. The dangerous nature of mining with its team work, each man depending on the others for his safety, meant strong bonds were forged between men and their families too. A close-knit community evolved in a self-sufficient village where all lived within sight of the winding gear of the pit shaft. Businesses grew up to cater for the needs of a fast growing population; it was said there was nothing you could not get from either Walter Wilsons, Broughs or the Co-op.

Churches were built for the spiritual needs of the various denominations of Methodists, Catholics and Anglicans. The Parish Church of St Mary's is often called 'The Miners' Cathedral'.

Social life too revolved around their work. The Miners' Welfare Hall was the venue for dances, visiting theatre groups, variety and musical shows. The miners' recreation ground had bowling greens, a bandstand for the colliery band and football pitches for the colliery team. Though some miners preferred the handball courts, whippet racing or even games of 'pitch and toss' on the beach banks.

During the Depression life was very hard for many households struggling to bring up large families of children. There was always a sinking feeling when the pit buzzer blew, heralding another week of short time work for the men and desperate straits for their women who had to feed their children. The buzzer, when heard between shifts, meant even worse news – an accident of some kind. Although Horden colliery did not have any major disaster, not many families escaped at least one member injured or even killed in the course of his work.

The coking plant was opened during the Depression, and considerations like conservation of the coastline were of very secondary importance then. The dumping of waste over the beach banks may have rendered the beaches black and useless for leisure, but it meant much needed work for the menfolk.

During the Second World War mining was a reserved occupation, but

Horden Colliery, now demolished

no soft option to life in the army. Some miners volunteered for the Forces and 'Bevin Boys' came to man the pits.

After Nationalisation in 1947 there began to be better pay and conditions for miners. This, combined with the need for coal to power the country's regeneration after the war, brought more prosperous times. The children they had struggled to bring up in the 1920s and 1930s had now grown to manhood, bringing in additional wages for families and becoming assets to the household. The coal seams went out under the sea and at its furthest men were working 5 to 6 miles out under the seabed extracting coal.

There was time for fun too. Many families had resident caravans or wooden chalets at Crimdon Dene and Happy Valley a few miles south down the coast where days, weekends and 'miners' fortnight' could be spent. The Dene would be filled to capacity with families enjoying seeing the local Beauty Queen chosen on August Bank Holiday Monday. Famous Labour leaders were invited to speak, colliery bands played and a great time was had by all. 'Mannie' Shinwell, their popular MP for Easington District for many years often addressed the crowds. It was a local joke that his votes were weighed, not counted! And of course there was Durham Gala Day when men from all the Durham collieries paraded in the city under their banners.

The New Town of Peterlee, built a couple of miles inland in the brave new world of post war planning, marked the first exodus of the younger generation from the village. They preferred the then ultra-modern houses of 'Windy City' to the solid old terraces of their parents.

Today the pit is closed. Only the wheel of the winding gear, set in a plaque opposite the site where the pit head baths once stood, is left to show that there was ever a colliery here. The spoil heaps are flattened and landscaped, and nature is beginning to repair the ravaged beaches. The younger generation of miners, like their grandfathers before them, have migrated to where miners are still needed. The rest hope that new factories and industries will come to occupy the land between Horden and the sea where once stood the reason for its existence – Horden colliery.

Howden-le-Wear

Howden-le-Wear is part of the parish of Fir Tree and lies on the road between Crook and Bishop Auckland. The parish was formed in 1862 and had a population of 2,426. Howden alone, now has 2,085 inhabitants. In the 1860s the village began to grow with the opening of the collieries, and the inhabitants were mostly the men working in the collieries and their families. Since the wars the village has been enlarged with new housing estates, flats and private houses.

The junior and infant school is built behind the original one, which is now a well-used community centre. The church of St Mary the Virgin stands well back from the main road, and is not easily seen. The Methodist Chapel stands on the right of the main road on the way to Bishop Auckland. Both were built with the village in 1869 and 1870 respectively, and both are well attended. There is a good variety of shops, a post office and five pubs, including an hotel.

In 1511 there was a large house built in its own grounds belonging to the Bowes family. For three centuries it was the home of the Coates family. In 1847, Smelt House was built over the site of the old house. In the right side is a brick from the original house bearing the arms of the Bowes family and the date 1511. Alas, the house, after being used for several purposes, is now a remand home.

We have our own Women's Institute Hall, built in 1925 on land given to the institute by Mrs Fryer who lived in Smelt House for many years. Every year a garden party was held in the grounds, with the children dancing round the maypole. The proceeds went to the Women's Institute.

The village is in a shallow dip, and most roads lead uphill out of the village. It is not a great distance from the dales, and as the crow flies, from the Scottish border. Before modern roads were built the drovers brought their livestock over the hills from the dales and Scotland, through Howden, which was then only fields, farms and farm cottages dotted here and there. Of course, there were rustlers of sheep, and a gibbet was erected to hang the rustlers when caught. The gibbet stood at the crossroads near what is now known as Gibbet's Hill Farm on Gibbet's Hill, along Douglas Lane. Some people say that a certain old original cottage, where a family called Howe lived, was a hiding place for the rustlers when they were being hunted, and was called Howe's Den. Hence the name of the village, Howden. There is also talk of the ghost of Lady Douglas who lived at The Towers in the next village, wandering across the fields to Howden every New Year's Eve. She had been murdered somewhere in the vicinity. She has not been seen for many years.

A railway ran through Howden, chugging up to Tow Law to the north and south-east to Darlington, linking with the train from the dales at Wear Valley Junction. The bridge over the line at Howden is now standing over the line at Beamish Museum. Part of the area where the railway line ran has been made into a children's playground.

Jubilee Park stands at the south end, with a stream running through it. The park was named after Queen Victoria's Jubilee. It was used for the annual Horticultural show, which was very popular and attracted people from a wide area. The remains of the bandstand are there as a reminder of the shows, with their music and entertainment.

Howden has a Wesleyan Chapel standing in the High Street, which was unused for many years, until it was bought by the founders of The North East Theatre Organ Association. They had decided that the theatre organs of the north east were fast disappearing, and something had to be done about it. Funds were raised and the chapel renovated to accommodate one of these beautiful organs. There are regular concerts, with guest artists from all over the country and the world. The Wurlitzer has certainly put Howden on the map.

In a cottage in the village there once lived an eccentric, kindly man, who had a pony and cart. The pony slept in the house with him. He decided that the pony needed a new cart, so he made one himself, in the house, but when it was completed he found he couldn't get it out.

Howden is an active village, with a Women's Institute, Mothers' Union, Scouts, Brownies, Youth Club, and organ concerts. There are dancing sessions and carpet bowls. Every year a leek show is held and the proceeds go towards the 'Old People's Treat'. This is usually held in May, and they are given a meal and some form of entertainment.

Most people travel out daily to work in the larger towns, but there are quite a number who work in the local shops, garage, nearby farms and the building trade. There are many interesting walks to surrounding villages, along quiet paths away from the main road. There are lovely views of the hills in the distance, fields with sheep and cattle, and horses. Birds are everywhere with their individual colour and song. Every season brings something new to find in the hedges.

Howden is a very interesting and friendly place to live.

Hurworth

Hurworth, a pretty village, is situated three miles south of Darlington on the north side of the river Tees. Formerly it was the home of a small community of linen weavers and agriculturalists.

Entering from the west end, you pass a fountain commemorating the accession of George V in 1911. Behind this is the old Village School now imaginatively converted into dwelling houses. The road continues through the village, passing on the right the village green, which is backed by attractive 18th and early 19th century houses. These face equally good houses fronted by a narrow tree lined green; number 24 being the site of the home of William Emmerson, 1701–1782. He was the renowned and eccentric mathematician – son of a former village schoolmaster. Wall sundials on some of these houses are attributed to him.

A little further down the village is Hurworth House Preparatory School for boys, and beyond this is the first of three hostelries – The Bay Horse, opposite which stands All Saints Church. Two lych gates lead into the graveyard where you will find Emmerson's Tomb. Inside the church are fine examples of Frosterley Marble, and stained glass windows.

At the east end of the village are more old cottages dating back to 1715, on one of which an original fire mark can be seen. Here also is the Temperance Hall still used by many village organisations, including the Women's Institute.

Passing the two remaining hostelries – The Emmerson Arms, and the Otter and Fish, we come to an iron bridge. Privately owned, it was built in the 1800s.

Whilst in recent years there has been much new development in the village, including the conversion of a large house into a thriving Community Centre, Hurworth remains an unspoilt, friendly village, of many greens, sundials, river views, trees, and attractive doorcasings.

Ireshopeburn

Ireshopeburn is a small village named after the tributary of the river Wear, which flows at its western end. It is a pretty village, set amongst the foothills of the northern Pennines in an area of outstanding natural beauty. Its stone built cottages are mostly set at the side of the road in irregular groups interspersed with meadow and pasture, with trees planted by the highway and many wooden troughs of flowers cared for by the inhabitants.

Many wild flowers grow by the river paths and in the meadows, organically farmed, on either side of the road to Newhouse.

Ireshopeburn was once part of the Forest of Weardale, hunting ground for the Prince Bishops of Durham. After the enclosure of the lower part of the forest between Westgate and Eastgate as a deer park during the 13th century the agricultural development of the High Forest began, first with shielings where cattle were brought for summer grazing and later, as the land was cleared and pasture and meadowland enclosed by farms that were occupied throughout the year. By 1300 there were four of these shielings in what is now Ireshopeburn, – Gate, Earnwell, Papworth Hill and Hole. Mining in upper Weardale, for lead, iron and silver, goes back even further than the development of agriculture. Lead and iron were mined in the hills around Ireshopeburn and as far back as 1527 there were miners living in the village. Lead mining reached its peak in the mid 19th century. In 1854 the Newhouse School was built on land given by W. B. Beaumont, lessee of the Weardale mines, at a cost of £1,400. £900 was given by W. B. Beaumont and £500, raised by subscription, every miner in work contributing 10/-. The school fees of miner's children (4d. per week in 1877) were paid by the Lead Company. This building is now a hotel–restaurant named 'The Ranch'.

In 1883 the mines were taken over by the Weardale Lead Company, with workshops in Ireshopeburn, now occupied by Featherstone Bros. Agricultural Engineers, and offices incorporating the cottage known as Wesley Garth. The manager lived in Weardale House rebuilt in 1916 and now used as a youth centre by the YMCA.

John Wesley paid his first visit to Ireshopeburn in 1752, preaching under a thorn tree. A commemorative plaque has been placed in a field near the chapel. High House Chapel, the chapel high in the dale, was built in 1760, the first Methodist Church in Weardale. It is the second oldest Methodist Church in England still in use.

An adjoining house for the minister was built in 1804 and the chapel enlarged in 1872. The former minister's dwelling now houses the Weardale Museum. Restored by the Community Task Force in 1984 and managed by a group of volunteers, the Museum includes the Weardale room, furnished as a late 19th century lead miner's living room, the Wesley room and displays on rocks, minerals and mines, railways, farming, water, industry, landscape and wild-life, all pertaining to Weardale.

Coronation Bridge, built to celebrate the Coronation of Queen Victoria crosses the Wear at the east end of the village where a road leads up to Newhouse. Before the building of the bridge the river was crossed by a ford, the road to which led down through what is now the garden of Coronation Cottage. This was once the gate house for a level crossing, the gates of which can still be seen on either side of the road.

In 1978 another bridge was built by British Steel across the Wear to serve the processing plant. This plant is now closed, bringing further unemployment to the Dale. At the west end of the village, on the road to Wearhead, an iron bridge crosses the Ireshopeburn. An older stone bridge known as Dallison's Bridge, crosses the burn on the road to Lanehill. Near this bridge is a cottage which was once a Presbyterian Chapel, built in 1687. By 1720 there were 150 members of the congregation, drawn from Kilhope, Wellhope and Ireshopeburn. The first Presbyterians in Weardale may have been Scottish Covenanters, escaping from religious persecution.

July 17th 1983 is a date the inhabitants of Ireshopeburn will never forget. A sudden storm over Noon Hill, in the watershed between upper Teesdale and Weardale, resulted in a flash flood. Rainfall of 104.8 mm was recorded on Ireshope plains between 14.30 and 17.00 GMT. Large areas of fell-side were stripped of heather and peat, debris was swept down the Ireshopeburn and piled up against Dallison's Bridge. The burn burst its banks and water found its way into old mines, coming up again near Low Burn Caravan Site. The people escaped to higher ground but one caravan was swept away and split in half on the sewage pipe, from which sewage escaped into the river for the next six weeks. Many houses in Ireshopeburn were flooded and farmers left to re-build stream banks and replace fences, the Northumbrian Water Authority refusing to accept responsibility for a tributary of the Wear. An action group was formed to compile a detailed account of the disaster and appeals for help. No help was forthcoming but the village was awarded second prize in Durham Village Ventures Competition.

In 1890 there were two grocers and drapers in Ireshopeburn (one with a post office) a butcher, a tailor, a boot and shoe maker, two joiners and two blacksmiths. A hundred years later there are no shops and no post office. The forge is now the home and workshop of the Cromptons, spinners and weavers. Next to Forge Cottage is the Institute, built in 1897 the year of Queen Victoria's Diamond Jubilee. It is the scene of many village functions, for although the population of Ireshopeburn has declined, some of its cottages used as holiday homes and a high proportion of its residents retired, there is still a strong community spirit in this pleasant Weardale village.

Iveston

Tucked away almost out of sight except for a view in silhouette from the Leadgate by-pass and the A691 from Lanchester, Iveston is a residential area with long history. There are various records of the name – and probably the modern one is closest to Ive's Stone – the stone on which St Ivo is said to have preached. St Ivo, according to legend, is said to have been a Persian archbishop who came to preach to the Roman soldiers – Iveston is on Dere Street and in line with Lanchester and Ebchester on Agricola's road.

Saxon settlements were called 'ton' or 'tun' which maybe is another explanation.

The Parish church in nearby Leadgate is dedicated to St Ive.

Thanks to the great historical record, the Boldon Book, we learn that in 1183 the Manor was called upon to pay two marks, provide a milch cow, plough one acre and a half of the Lords land at Lanchester, attend the great chase with two greyhounds and undertake the carriage of wine with a wain of eight oxen.

Later the land became the property of Kepier hospital in Durham and after 1537 when the monasteries were dissolved, it came eventually to the Tempest family.

An early co-operative was founded when it was decreed that every man would contribute to the sinking of a 'cole pit' in 1611 and those who refused 'shall have no part of ye coles gotten there'.

Coal was first taken from pittes or groves and miners delved for it. Traditional coal mining was indigenous in the eastern side of Durham and gradually it spread so that there were so many seams that pit falls today might reveal the existence of pits whose names are long forgotten.

Pits at Iveston were small and the yield generally served the local people. The Iveston pit of any substance was sunk in 1950 by the Consett Iron Company closing in 1892.

It is recorded that a pit called St Ives closed – it lay between Iveston and the Brooms on the eastern outskirts of Leadgate village and had in 1728 a Newcomen engine.

Nearby is evidence of a more recent trait in coal production – open cast mining where land is now being allowed to subside naturally after being mechanically upturned to allow surface mining to take place – a phenomena which took place on a small scale all those centuries ago.

Modern Iveston is a residential area which retains its agricultural facade and a stud where Hanoverian horses are bred and a crop of blue lupins recently attracted some attention as an experiment away from the acid yellow fields of oil seed rape which light up the Spring countryside.

Kelloe

Kelloe village is known to have had Bronze Age residents. A grave containing the five partially burned skeletons of a family and a bronze age beaker were found some fifty years ago.

Many people do not know of Kelloe church being the place of baptism for Elizabeth Barrett Browning born at nearby Coxhoe Hall. She was christened Elizabeth Barrett on February 10th 1808 before the family moved to Herefordshire a few months later.

Buried in the churchyard are 26 victims of the 74 men and boys who lost their lives in the Trimdon Grange Colliery disaster in 1882.

The local mines and Coxhoe Hall are now gone, as has been the fate of many colliery communities. The Norman church still stands sentinel over the scattered Parish.

St Helen's Church, Kelloe

Lanchester

Lanchester lies in the valley, surrounded by hills, once forested, eight miles north of Durham. The name derives from the Roman Fort, Longovicium, and an ornamental inscribed slab now in the Dean & Chapter Library at Durham, indicates that it was built in AD 140 by the Twentieth Legion at about the same time as Hadrian's Wall.

The Fort remains largely unexcavated and the site has been in possession of the Greenwells, a well-known local family, since 1633. Dr William Greenwell, historian, archaeologist, & inventor of the famous fishing fly Greenwell's Glory, whose ancestors earlier appear in the Boldon Book, is buried in the churchyard.

Discoveries of tumuli (ancient burial mounds) at Maiden Law, and an arrowhead, a stone axe, a bust of a Celtic God, bear witness to the occupation of the area by tribes of Ancient Britons, probably the Brigantes, who favoured hilltops for their strongholds.

There is also evidence of Saxon occupation in the area; a farmer fishing in the Smallhope Burn at Hurbuck unearthed a hoard of weapons including a sword, four scythes and eight axeheads.

Old villagers talk of the Seven Wells of Lanchester, eg Kitswell, Chapmans Well, Prospect, and one old character, Dick Gallon, who was manservant to old Dr Wilson of Park House, could be seen every morning with a yoke on his shoulder carrying two pails of spring water from the well in the Halves. The present by-pass road built in 1972, cut through the Halves but the spring is still in use there in the grounds of the Lodge, a listed Georgian house at the foot of the hillside which forms a beautiful backdrop to the village.

The modern village has grown in recent times – from the 1851 records of 150 houses and 752 inhabitants, the number has risen to approximately 6,000 today. It still has a farming community, but since the 1960s outlying fields have been sold to developers.

Entering Lanchester from the south we first see the Parish Church of All Saints, a typical Norman church begun in 1147 and the Monolithic columns on the north side of the Nave are Roman and no doubt came from the colonnade of the headquarters building. In the church porch there is an altar dedicated to the Goddess Garmangabis, found near a spring on Margery Flats Farm. It bears an inscription thought to confirm the name of the Roman camp Longovicium.

In 1939 new pews were made for the church by Robert 'mouse' Thompson of Kilburn, and his special trademark can be found by visitors who wish to search.

The King's Head public house and small hotel sits opposite the church, and behind it, for many years, the local mart served farmers and butchers who came from miles around. The last session was held in 1973, and local pubs were allowed to open all day.

The Green, now owned by the Parish Council, dominates the centre of the village with its attractive Sycamore and Copperbeech trees underplanted with daffodils.

In 1819 a small Methodist Chapel was built by public subscription on the village green, but later when newer buildings took over, the chapel became a blacksmiths shop. The smith at one time was George Jackson, who made ironwork for the north door of the parish church. Front Street curves gently around the western side of the green and although most of the old houses have gone, it still retains its village feel.

One of the interesting old houses in Lanchester is Ornsby Hill House

Front Street, Lanchester as it was in the early 1900s

built about 1778; it has wells in the house and garden, and a funeral chute for bringing coffins downstairs.

Being in the valley, Lanchester is well supplied with burns, as they are known, and on many occasions in the past the village has been flooded but now they have been culverted. Several mills sprang up, and The Old Mill Cottage is inhabited today.

Not far away from here, in 1922, a memorial hall in remembrance of the dead of the First World War was built and in 1925 the first meeting of the Women's Institute was held here. After seeing life as a Labour Exchange and then the Empress Cinema, the site has now a well built block of flats for the elderly, with central courtyard and gardens.

One resident remembers that just after the First World War, each September an Irishman, known as 'the goose man', would appear in the village with a hundred or more geese. These he would keep on the village green and by Christmas they would all be sold.

The branch railway which opened in 1862 was one of the busiest places in the village and excursions to Newcastle and Sunderland for 1/3d were very popular – visitors would come to sit on the green and walk in the fields.

On the annual occasion of the Durham Miners Gala, the 'Big Meeting', miner's lodges from surrounding places would walk with their band and banners to the station to catch the train to Durham. After closing in 1965 the railway has now become the Derwent Valley Walk, with picnic sites and information points. It attracts many walkers, cyclists and visitors all year round. One car park and entrance to the walk is not far from where the old workhouse was erected in 1839 and early records show that young people and children lived together with old people, their day beginning at 5 am and ending at 8 pm. One hundred years later the workhouse became Lee Hill Hospital for the old and infirm and thirty years on again it has become a small housing estate, Lee Hill Court.

Over the years the various seasons and festivals were always celebrated in the village. As Easter approached Carlin Sunday, the Sunday before Palm Sunday, was celebrated by the consumption of quantities of grey peas called carlins; thought to have been brought to Newcastle upon Tyne by ship when that city was under siege. Carlin Sunday commemorated that event. Public houses would sell them cooked for a penny. Also at Easter dyed eggs were a common sight, there being great competition to see who could produce the prettiest ones dyed with onion peels, lichen, or rags. On Easter Monday children would go to the top of the hill known as Pasch Egg Bank, now Paste Egg, and roll down their eggs running merrily after them. Boys would try to 'jarp' or knock them. Although this custom died out long ago, this bank, when covered with snow is still used by children and adults for sledging.

Leadgate

As the name suggests – Lead and tolls – combined to give this satellite village of the town of Consett, its name. Lead was transported on ponies from Weardale to the Tyne, and the tollgate is believed to have barred straight passage. Where exactly the toll stood is the subject for conjecture. In 1749 there was said to be just one inhabited house on this route which lay between Consett and Dipton. The pack route must have crossed Dere Street north of Iveston which was part of the Lanchester parish until St Ives Church was established in 1863. North West Durham seems to have been a safe haven for many European refugees and it is said that monks from Douai in Northern France set up a community at Pontop Hall near Dipton in 1784 for six emigrees before they moved to Crookhall near Consett, and subsequently to Ushaw where the celebrated college was founded.

In 1844 there were two reasons for celebration; the Leadgate vicarage was built, and the Eden Colliery was sunk – it survived some 120 years. The site is now carved out as a maze on the Consett to Sunderland cycle path.

An unhappy ghost of a woman is said to stalk between the nearby Jolly Drovers pub and the village – thought to be the unhappy Lady Dunn who is thought to have been deprived of her inheritance. Two 'Dunn' names crop up, Margaret Tempest Dunn landowner and Rev George Hames Dunn whose address was given as Charnwood House in Leicestershire. The land on which the vicarage was built was of the estate of Cuthbert Dunn, 1843. Which denomination built the vicarage is unclear as it was not until 1863 that the Parish of Leadgate was formed.

Until the area outside became a burial ground, coffins had to be carried the four miles to Lanchester for interment.

Brooms Dene, once a beauty spot is long gone – filled in as a rubbish tip by Derwentside district council.

A stop on the passenger line which ran from Blackhill, through the Consett Iron Works (once an awesome sight – like Blake's satanic mills) via Consett, to Newcastle, Leadgate was a thriving community at the cross roads of roads from Durham and Tyneside.

Now the passenger and mineral lines have ceased, the village is bypassed by all but local traffic, little remaining of its industrial heritage, and none of the significance it once held.

Low Middleton

Low Middleton is now a small hamlet comprising seven dwellings, its only public amenity a letter-box in the boundary wall of Low Middleton Hall. In medieval times it was a much larger village and signs of earlier habitation were visible in the fields North of Low Middleton until some

The Dovecot, Low Middleton

twenty years ago. Still surviving from a later period is a large octagonal dovecote with mellow brick walls, pantiled roof and over 1,500 nesting holes. This stands in one of the fields to the South of Low Middleton Hall near the river Tees.

Low Middleton Hall is believed to have been the Manor House for many years before the present house was completed in 1721. The downcomers bear the initials R. J. K. for Robert and Jane Killinghall, who built the house or possibly only altered it and made the garden front, a very pleasing combination of red brick and sandstone. Jane Killinghall died not long afterwards and is buried in the nearby St George's Church. The house changed hands many times. Perhaps the most notable occupier being H. A. W. Cocks, known as Squire Cocks, who built on a Victorian tower on the North side of the house and also a tower which has since fallen down at the West end of St George's Church. Major Ralph Turton bought the house about 50 years ago and it is still owned by his daughter. It is in use as a guest house by the present tenant.

Walkers along the recently-designated Teesdale Way riverside footpath pass close to Low Middleton and can appreciate its air of rural charm.

Medomsley

At the time of the Boldon Book, which was Bishop Pudsey's answer to the Domesday Book, Medomsley was a free Manor paying rent to the Prince Bishops.

Later much of the land was owned by the Surtees family of Hamsterley Hall near Burnopfield. (The Surtees family were also connected with the other Hamsterley in Weardale and their name crops up frequently in the county).

A century ago a number of Celtic spear heads were found by a ploughman at High Bradley farm.

Cromwell's army also passed through the village camping overnight – mentioned in the Boldon Book was the Manor – and the church register dates back to 1608. For many years the Manor House was used as a lodging house for the Judges at the Assizes and Police motor cycle outriders used to accompany the limousine from the village.

Twice in the early part of this century tragedy struck at Medomsley. In 1911 when a charabanc load of happy choristers on their way to compete in a music festival at Prudhoe, the brakes failed and it hurtled out of control to the bottom of the bank. Ten members of the Consett Co-operative Choir were killed, nine at the scene, another in hospital, and 23 were either hurt or badly shaken. The second, in 1923 was more typical of a mining community when eight men died as the pit cage in which they were travelling from their shift underground hit something and plunged downward, throwing five of the men to the bottom of the shaft. The three others were found lying on top of the corresponding cage which had been descending empty.

During the General strike in 1926 village children were given free soup at the Stag pub – just one of the many instances when the produce from local allotments came in handy.

Two mines were sunk in this rural village, the Cromwell which had two seams, the Top Busty and the Brockwell, and the Derwent sunk in 1853. They are long since closed but they once jointly employed some 1,000 men and boys.

Medomsley cricket team still survives in the village which is now a dormitory area on the outskirts of Consett. Neighbouring Allendale Cottages is left to memory with only the former doctor's house and the Institute building remaining. Between Allendale and Medomsley lies the housing estate called 'The Dene'.

Middleton In Teesdale

The name Middleton means middle farm or settlement and 'in Teesdale' was added more than 700 years ago, to differentiate it from others of the same name in County Durham.

The village suffered in the latter part of the 11th century when William the Conqueror bid to waste much of the land, and the Scots also raided Teesdale, and, in a battle at Hunderwaite in 1070, a number of English noblemen were killed. William Rufus granted Middleton and other lands to Guy de Baliol in 1093 and his family held the estate for the next 200 years. In 1632 the estate was bought by Sir Henry Vane and has remained in his family. The present Lord Barnard owns some houses in the village (eg. White Row) and the office of the Upper Teesdale agent is in Middleton.

Farming has always been a way of life in Upper Teesdale and remains so today. The land is too high for arable farming and now there is little dairying. Suckler herds are kept and the almost ubiquitous Shorthorns of former years have been replaced by Limousins, Belgian Blues, Charollais and other breeds. Swaledale sheep have been bred for hundreds of years and are well suited to the harsh winter climate. Latterly Leicesters, Suffolks, cross-breds and even foreign sheep have been introduced. The Auction Mart at Middleton serves all the upper dale and is especially busy in the Autumn, with cattle and sheep sales, at which sometimes there are prizes for the best animals. The mart is also the venue for furniture sales and recently Mr Brent Stephenson, the present owner of Middleton House, sold furniture used by Prince Charles when he came grouse shooting as the guest of Sir Joseph Nickerson and gave the proceeds to charity.

We have another royal link – the Queen Mother and the then Duke of York spent part of their honeymoon at Holwick Mansion, owned by the Strathmore family.

Farming has shaped the landscape, together with lead-mining. The London Lead Company, of Quaker origin, operated in the dale from 1753–1905, and there were several mines around Middleton. Today there only remains the spoil heaps and derelict buildings. The Company showed concern for its workers and encouraged thrift and sobriety. Houses were built in Middleton graded according to the status of the workmen whose families would occupy them; from the humble cottages in Ten Row (River Terrace) to the imposing detached residence, Middleton House, where the agent lived. One of the agents was Robert Walton Bainbridge, who presented a fountain (near the car park) bought with money from a testimonial to him. Miners worked hard in very primitive and dangerous conditions and many died young. One of the most notable lead miners, a poet by inclination and a miner by hard necessity, was Richard Watson, the Teesdale poet, the centenary of whose death was remembered in 1981. A handsome wooden plaque can be seen in the window of the Mechanics Institute. The Lead Company opened a school in Alston Road in 1861 and Sabbath Schools were held in the Chapels. The withdrawal of the Company in 1905 brought great hardship to the Upper Dale.

The coming of the North Eastern Railway in 1868 opened up the dale to tourists coming to see the flowers, birds and animals and to enjoy the scenery. England's Last Wilderness draws more visitors every year – generating some income locally, but causing some problems, especially car-parking. The Pennine Way runs up the valley on the south side of the Tees.

Today there are a few small industrial units in the village providing some jobs, but many people work at Glaxo at Barnard Castle. There is a good community spirit in the dale and interesting activities are available for people of all ages. Middleton is a pleasant place to live – the shopkeepers are courteous and helpful, the people are friendly, and the scenery, at all seasons of the year, is very beautiful. Anyone who has seen the dale in a snowy Winter or noted the variety of flowers in the hay meadows in early summer will retain happy memories of Middleton and Upper Teesdale.

Middleton St George & Middleton One Row

The village now known as Middleton St George developed from one of three medieval settlements by the river Tees. Few traces remain of the other two. The whole area contained only one church, dedicated to St George – hence the name of the village. This ancient church is still used for a monthly Evensong Service and is the parish burial ground.

The old Roman road from York to Newcastle crossed the Tees on Pountey's Bridge, long since gone, though the name survives in Pountey's Close on the Council estate. A significant date in its development is 1789. While excavations for coal were going on in woodland near the boundary with Low Dinsdale, a sulphurous spring was discovered. Its waters were found to have medicinal properties and a Spa grew up, which became quite famous and was responsible for the growth of Middleton One Row at that time, all traces of the medieval houses having long disappeared.

1825 is an even more important date. The Railway Age can be said to have really started with the opening of the Stockton and Darlington Railway. The line passed through the north of the parish and a station was built and named after the adjacent inn, The Fighting Cocks. The railway greatly improved access to the Spa and in his *Home Tour* of 1837, Sir George Head speaks of being 'speedily consigned by a steam carriage on the Darlington Railroad, which deposited me at The Fighting Cocks.'

The existence of the Railway had stimulated the rapid creation of Middlesbrough as an ironworks town. Around 1860, blast furnaces were set up in Middleton. There followed an urgent need for labour and housing. Many workers had to be recruited from outside including some from Ireland. The ironworkers' houses were mainly built in long rows and still stand today. Modernised and well maintained, they make an attractive entrance to the village from the north.

Wire mills and ironworks followed the blast furnaces and Middleton St George grew rapidly. 75% of the village existing at the end of the Second World War was built between 1860 and 1900. Industrialists, managers and professional men were naturally involved in its development and the road by the river was an obvious choice for the superior housing required. These houses, with their differing architectural styles, still exist today in Middleton One Row.

Owing to the expansion during this period, the old church had become entirely unsuitable both in size and location and in 1871 a new church dedicated to St Laurence was built at the junction of Middleton St George and 'The One Row'. The stone Saxon sundial from St George's Church is now kept in St Laurence's. Sixteen years later, with the re-alignment of the railway, a new passenger station was built and given the name Dinsdale, to add to the confusion of names within the village.

Increases in population in the early part of this century were gradual until the construction, about a mile away, of a Royal Air Force aerodrome and servicemen's quarters at the beginning of the war. This brought almost a thousand new residents to the village. Military administration at the airfield was relinquished in 1964 and it is now a modern International Airport – thus continuing the theme of transport, which has been such a significant feature of the growth of Middleton St George.

So much for past history; what of the village now? For the residents, it has much to offer. There are four pubs and two hotels; a flourishing Social and Cricket Club; a Community Centre equipped for water sports and other physical activities; a Post Office and a range of shopping facilities; a Women's Institute and organisations for the young. There is also a school and a Methodist Church. Visitors' interests are also covered with a thriving golf club and a regional Tennis Centre. There is a convalescent home in a delightful setting; no fewer than three retirement homes and Trees Park retirement village. The village is well served by all forms of public transport – bus, train and plane.

In spite of a considerable degree of urbanisation, Middleton St George has retained much of its rural character and is still a green and pleasant place in which to live.

Neasham

Visitors to Neasham, a village 4 miles south of Darlington, find an attractive mixture of old cottages and modern houses running along a curve of the river Tees from which it is protected by a raised flood-bank. This provides a footpath from which to enjoy the view of the widening river and the sheltering ridge of higher land and wooded slopes east of the village. Its other attraction is the Fox and Hounds, a 19th century public house, with a modern dining room and conservatory, large car-park and a very popular adventure playground. With its darts and dominoes and quiz nights as well as a generous cook, it is an obvious centre of entertainment for the whole neighbourhood. Of the 18th century cottages on either side, one used to house a dame-school and the other was the ferryman's house. A right-of-way between pub and Boat-house down to the river is all that is left of the ferry, where the boat was dragged down when required.

The houses continue in an irregular line from No 1 to 91 facing the river but the even numbers are interrupted by the green. In 1902 Sir Thomas Wrightson, owner of Neasham Hall, a palladian mansion on Sockburn Lane, tidied that corner at the crossroads by replacing a muddle of old cottages, privies and pigsties with a group of well-built estate houses, detached, double-fronted, with large sash windows and front gardens, unusual in a village where cottages mostly opened onto the pavement, with land behind for vegetables, fruit and livestock. Their windows had always been small-paned sliding Yorkshire Lights. Round Sockburn Lane corner were two semi-detached buildings, but opening either front door revealed a hall, to be the Reading Room where the estate provided newspapers for the village men to read there. It was so designed that if it proved an unnecessary provision it could easily be transformed into two estate houses. Never any need for that! The Reading Room has been fully used ever since. During the First World War the army commandeered it, and a service-oak was planted outside to commemorate the peace. Meantime in 1916 the newly-formed Women's Institute had to meet in an old railway carriage on the other corner where the road climbs up to Middleton-St-George. A row of bungalows was built there in the 1970s.

Reading continued as part of the hall's function as it housed the County Branch Library until it was superseded by the Mobile Library

Service in 1952. Since then, while retaining the name, the Reading Room has been a full-fledged village hall, generously donated to the village by the Wrightsons in 1955, to be run by an elected management committee, and funded by the levy of a small membership fee from every villager, as well as by fund-raising efforts and hiring to various groups and for individual parties. The committee runs weekly whist and domino drives and a coffee and chat morning. The WI meets there for an annual rent, paying extra for fund-raising.

The other arm of the cross-roads is Neasham Hill, climbing steeply before it descends to river level in Low Middleton. Dominating the hill is positively the oldest house in the village, an elegant manor Neasham Hill House built in 1757 for the Wards who had owned a share of Neasham Manor since it was seized by the queen from the Durham Palatinate in 1577 and sold in 3 parts. All the villagers retreated to Neasham Hill in 1771 when the Hurworth rector, Rev Bramwell, galloped through the villages warning everyone as far as Yarm of an approaching wall of water sweeping down the Tees. Everyone in Neasham survived but all the houses, crops and livestock were swept away, leaving only Neasham Hill House untouched. They rebuilt their cottages sturdily after that, using cobbles and gravel from the river, facing the thick untidy walls with pebble-dash or neat local bricks and roofing them with red clay pantiles from the local tile-works.

At the foot of the Hill stands the ornate Pumphouse, the gift of Rowland Ward in 1879. The other public pump was built opposite the Fox and Hounds to commemorate Queen Victoria's Golden Jubilee in 1887 but only a date and the initials JP remain to mark the spot and mystify visitors.

Except for occasional additions (eg the Fox and Hounds and a school in 1870) the village kept this appearance until the 1960s. It was officially being allowed to decay, classified Category D after 1945 because there was no mains-drainage, though piped water and communal taps had replaced most pumps by the First World War and gas and electricity reached the village in the early 1930s. In 1958 the Golden Cock, a homely little tavern in a terrace of cottages at the east end, was closed, and in 1960 the school had dwindled to 29 pupils, so its closure was sad but unsurprising.

Then in 1964 the difficulties caused by floods and springs were overcome – mains-drainage was installed and new building permitted. Derelict cottages and Golden Cock were demolished, gardeners were tempted to sell their suddenly valuable land and the village street filled with new housing. Some old cottages were carefully restored, the school as a house, retained its old shape. The Hare and Hounds, now a double-fronted cottage in the terrace facing the green, was the headquarters of the notorious Neasham Gang of highwaymen who terrorised travellers in the 16th century, rebuilt in 1771. Remains of its brewhouse and stabling have also been preserved. A little further along were two single-storey cottages which had been the Methodist chapel from 1796 to the 1890s, but these and the next door cottage were replaced by 1980 by a terrace of four upside down houses with upstairs sittingrooms to enjoy the view. The village shops had gradually been reduced to one quaint one-storey general store and post office, and by the end of the 1980s that had also gone.

Dependent on Hurworth for shops, post office, doctor and church, Neasham seems a mere hamlet compared with its neighbour a mile to the west, but it had great historical importance as the ford, the High Wath, was famous as the crossing of the Tees by the Great North Road. From 1203 to 1540 a Benedictine Abbey near the ford offered hospitality to travellers, the most famous being Princess Margaret, daughter of Henry VII, on her way to marry the king of Scotland. The 14th century Abbey Farm on the corner of the road to Darlington was part of the Abbey lands. After the Dissolution the abbey was demolished, the present house of that name being a mid-19th century mansion. Some stonework was moved for safety, including a 13th century cross, now in Durham Cathedral.

The ford was the scene of a special pageant on the inauguration of every Bishop of Durham. He was met midstream by the Lord of Sockburn who presented the falchion with which Sir John Conyers slew the Sockburn Worm. In 1790 the ford had been made unsafe by so much gravel needed in all the rebuilding, so the ceremony was moved to Croft Bridge. It lapsed after 1826 but was revived for the present Bishop. In 1800 a new wider and safer ford was built, the Low Wath, beside the ferry, though by this time the main road ran through Croft, and it is still in regular use by tractors. In 1968 the floodbank was built, blocking the High Wath, but a pathway for vehicles was devised to cross it at the Low Wath preserving the ford, a happy compromise, typical of the tolerant blend of old and new in Neasham.

Newbiggin-in-Teesdale

Newbiggin-in-Teesdale a now quiet little village is situated on the main road, and passed by many on their way to the well known and dramatic High Force Falls.

First mentioned before 1200 it was during the 18th and 19th centuries with the mining of lead by The London Lead Company, that it first came into prominence. Boys of 10 years old left school to work in the mines and earned 4p. per day to help eke out the family funds.

During this time several houses were built and the census of 1801 tells us that there were 281 inhabitants. However by 1861 the population had rapidly increased to 641 with 107 houses. Mining ceased by 1905 with only a short revival at Flushiemere during the Second World War years.

John Wesley is a name well known in Newbiggin-in-Teesdale as he preached in local houses before the Chapel was built in 1759, much of the work being done by the miners after a hard day's work. The money was mostly raised by local efforts.

The Sunday School and two flats above were added in 1882/3. During the period that the London Lead Company were involved in the area they gave much support and financial help, especially in the education of the children. A child leaving school at 10 years to work in mines had to first produce a certificate from the Sunday School Superintendent, a sure spur that the children were sent to Sunday School.

John Wesley visited 10 times and the pulpit from which he preached still stands in the Wesleyan Chapel. It is said to be the oldest chapel in the country still in continuous use where he preached. It houses an interesting collection of artefacts and is open every Wednesday from 2.00 to 4.30pm from April till the end of September.

Bowlees, a small hamlet nearby but within the parish of Newbiggin, had its own Methodist Chapel and in 1846 it held the first Sunday School in the Methodist Circuit. Near Bowlees there spanned the river Tees at Wynch Bridge what is said to have been the first suspension bridge in Europe, it was built in 1704. However, tragedy struck in 1802 when one of the main chains broke as 11 people were crossing and one person was drowned.

The school was established in 1799. The highest attendance period was in the 1880s when 127 children attended this small school. As the lead mines closed so attendances decreased and by 1952 there were only

25 children of all ages in the village so the school was closed. Children now have to be taken to the neighbouring larger village of Middleton-in-Teesdale and from 11 years old to Barnard Castle.

The village in its day had its own horse drawn hearse and Hearse House, library, lime kiln, blacksmiths' and village pub, its post office and its village shop, but all have now disappeared.

The village has had only one new house this century and the population is now 121. Farming is now the main industry with most of the smallholdings of previous years having been joined to larger farms to make them more viable.

Newsham

The origins of the village are lost in time, but it is likely that there were people living on the site in Roman times as a certain amount of Roman pottery has been found, which no doubt came from Roman troops and travellers using Watling Street which is still the northern boundary of the village.

The first hard fact about the village is the Domesday Book which states 'in Neuhusom – there are seven Carucates of Geld, and there may be 5 ploughs. Of this Ulchil had five Carucates and sport two Carucates and they had Halls. Now Earl Alan has the Land of Sport and Bodin the land of Ulchil and ten villans and four Bordars with four Ploughs. There are four Acrits of Meadow and Underwood, half a leuga in length and a third in bredth. The whole is one levea long and half broad'.

During Tudor and Stuart times the village must have prospered, as a market of some sort was held, the only remaining evidence is the old Market Cross at the west end of the village, together with the present iron stocks which replaced the old wooden ones in 1928.

In 1557 in the reign of Queen Mary the village or that part of it in the Ecclesiastical Parish of Kirkby Hill started to benefit from the founding of the free Grammar School, and Alms Houses by the Reverend John Dakyn at Kirkby Hill, and to this day the villagers can still benefit from what is known as the John Dakyn Trust, as the elderly who have lived in the Parish for at least 10 years can have the benefit of cheap accommodation, in one of the 6 flats in the Alms Houses as and when vacancies occur. Though the Grammar School no longer exists as a school the building is still there and exists as a flat and a meeting place, and money derived from the trust set aside to run the school is used to give grants to school leavers in the parish for further education.

During the Middle Ages the population of the village would have been employed in agriculture and in the many lead and coal mines on the moors to the south of the village.

There is little information then about the village until the writings of James Coates School Master of Newsham Place, who lived between 1761–1788. His journals are full of local detail. In this period there were two boarding schools, the afore-mentioned Newsham Place and Earby Hall, operated by the Johnson family, it appears that the schools were of the Dotheboys Hall type. These schools got their writing paper from the Newsham Paper Mill which operated on a site between the Corn Mill in the village and the Low Lane to Dalton and Gayles. Some remains of the Paper Mill still exist. The buildings that housed these schools are both still in existence.

In 1777 there was an Act of Parliament passed for 'dividing and enclosing the common and waste lands and a stinted pasture in the township of Newsham in the North Riding of the County of York.' The Act resulted in the Newsham Award on 3 June 1782 which is held in the Record Office at Northallerton. Two parts of this award are still in operation today, somewhat revised.

Again there is a scarcity of information until the 1890s when we have Bulmers *History and Directory of North Yorkshire* and a Minute Book of Village Meetings.

In 1890 Bulmer tells us that the village had – one general dealer, two grocers, one veterinary surgeon, one surgeon, one boot and shoe maker, one butcher, one tailor, one blacksmith and postmaster, one shepherd, one stonemason, three innkeepers and fifteen farmers.

Strangely no mention is made in Bulmer of a corn miller. In 1890, though, we know that the Corn Mill had been in operation for some considerable time.

On the 25th March, 1897 a Village Meeting decided to plant a tree on the village green to commemorate Queen Victoria's Diamond Jubilee. This tree was planted by Miss Millbank in the presence of Prince and Princess Radzwill and Princess Mary.

In the early 1900s the subject of piped water to houses in the village became an item at all the Parish Meetings. The problems associated with this took many years to resolve, and villagers continued to collect their water in pails and other containers from St Johns Well until 1930 when the Water Scheme led to piped water being installed in all houses.

1911 brought the Coronation of King George V and a Committee was formed in the village to arrange a fete to celebrate the event, and records show over 200 villagers attended, the cost amounting to £16.00.

Very little appears to have happened in the village during the Great War, apart from the Water Scheme, but in 1921 the War Memorial was erected at a cost of £174. The memorial was unveiled on 28 August, 1921 by Sir Fredrick Milbank.

1923 the Newsham Parish Meeting was granted the powers of a Parish Council to enable them to administer the village green. This was a Directive of the North Riding County Council.

Electricity came to the village in 1938. Mr Watson the Miller installed a generator in the Mill and had to ask permission to erect poles to carry light to his house.

1939 The GPO erected the first phone box on the village green, at an annual rate of one shilling.

During the 1930s there were many small businesses in the village – cornmill, cycle repair shop, selling tools and wetbattery charge service for wireless sets, boot and shoe maker, draper shop, seamstress, two blacksmiths and a wheelwright. Shops – one selling bread, cakes and tobacco, one post office selling tobacco cigarettes and groceries, a general store, three pubs and two haulage contractors.

A Bus Service was based in the village, and two other bus services passed through the village.

North Bitchburn

North Bitchburn lies on a rise between Howden and Bishop Auckland. Originally it was known as Beechburn, but no-one appears to know how or why it was changed to Bitchburn.

There are 59 houses at the moment, one Methodist chapel, a car repair garage, and a cricket club and cricket field with 1st and 2nd teams. The village shop closed in the 1960s. There is one public house, The Red Lion. The village was built between 1840 and 1857, with the discovery of coal. There was also a brick yard and pipe works. All now closed.

The view from the village is superb. Across the valley to Witton Castle and beyond to the Pennines, with undulating fields to the fore. Of course, there is nothing to stop the gales blowing over from the hills, and supplying good fresh air to all the inhabitants. Part of the Red Lion is 400 years old. It stands on the edge of the garth, a quite large paddock which was used for watering and resting animals overnight on their way to market in days gone by.

During the civil war, Cromwell's troops unhitched a cannon and gave Witton Castle, then a Royalist stronghold, a salvo of shot.

The village was used in a disguised form in the novel *The Earth Beneath* by H. Heslop.

There is a footpath through a field running steeply down to the main road below, which was used for grazing pit ponies. These ponies liked to chase anyone who happened to be hurrying down the field to catch a bus.

The houses have now nearly all been modernised. Most of the working population have to travel further afield for employment. They may have their own transport, but for those who have not, the bus passes through the village hourly to Bishop Auckland and Darlington and back to Crook and Tow Law. It is within walking distance of quite a few villages, making a pleasant form of exercise.

Oxhill

The name is derived from the hill on the road from East Kyo passing the Primitive Methodist Chapel. Over the crossing is the Ox Inn, formerly known as the Bull Inn. From 1863 to 1907 the landlord was John Errington, a well known sportsman. He was a tall man, with 'mutton chop' whiskers, a heavy snuff-taker and an inveterate smoker of cigars. He organised lots of sporting events in the fields behind the inn. The land was owned by Col Joicey and was then open land and not later intersected by the railway. As many as 2,000 people used to attend these events.

After the Ox Inn stood the old blacksmith's shop which used to be owned by Mr Jos Irwin. After his death the business closed due to the introduction of mechanical transport. Opposite stood a street of low stone built cottages known as Hedley Row and behind this row on the far side of the railway stood the derelict Oxhill engine which finished working in 1864. A little further along the same side are the whitewashed buildings of Oxhill Farm. Sixty years ago the tenant farmer was John Osbourne. One of his sons was a volunteer in the Consett troop of the Northumberland Hussars. He died in action and was given a military funeral. The funeral itself aroused much interest as it passed down Stanley Front Street. This is the only mention of a cavalryman's funeral in Stanley.

Going towards Stanley we pass along Joicey Terrace before reaching what is now the Oxhill Nursery School. The school was built in 1877 and stands on an eminence called Bessy Bell Hill. Who this lady was is not known but right opposite is a dwelling house with the name Bell Hill House. Leaving the school we next come to Pea Road on the left leading down to the Pea Farm. This farm is shown on old maps long before the first Ordnance Survey maps of 1856. Towards the end of 1908 a terrible crime was committed near this farm. Jeremiah O'Conner and Mary Donnelly (aged 11) disappeared from Stanley on 4th December, 1908. The body of the little girl was found in the far corner of the field behind the farm on Sunday morning December 20th. O'Conner was apprehended near Barcus Close by Inspector Start on December 19th and was in custody when the body of the victim was found. He was committed for trial and found guilty and sentenced to death. He paid the penalty for his crime in February 1909. O'Conner's execution passed almost unnoticed due to the dreadful disaster which took place at that time when the Burns Pit caught fire, bringing grief and bereavement to so many families in the town when 168 men and boys perished in the disaster. Near Oxhill is the Workmen's Club which is better known as the Arch Club. The road to the right leads to South Moor down Park Road, formerly known as Tommy's Lonnen, and the railway bridge (now removed) which was called Tommy's Arch. Going again towards Stanley we come to Louisa Terrace, first built in 1867. These houses were small and low and were rebuilt in 1894. The West Shield Row Pea Pit was approx 300 yards north west of Oxhill School. It was producing coal in 1779. The coal from this pit went by the Shield Row Waggonway to Beamish. The pit was deepened in 1831. The old waggonway from this pit to Beamish is still tracable in places and is known locally as the Black Road.

The Pea Pit closed in 1846 and in 1866 two constables, Marshall and Newbolt, were investigating the theft of a gamecock and three hens from the home of Mrs Mossom of Pea Pit Cottages when they discovered an illicit still. This was found when they searched the homes of two well known characters named Robins and Walton. They also found the missing fowls there. This is the only record of an illicit still in the Stanley area.

Oxhill Primitive Methodist Church came into being in 1873 when a band of men and women at Oxhill sought a place where they could worship. They were given a hut called Black's Cabin in the Oxhill pit yard. Such a 'church' in a coalmine yard had its disadvantages but these pioneers were not easily daunted. They met and sang their praises to God and forgot the discordant notes of industry. Others became interested and soon the cabin was too small and the move to a reading room was made. This had just been erected near the pit yard gates. Later, ground was obtained by Jane Luke, Tommy Fenwick and Robert Cordy from Lord Joicey and the foundation stone for the new church was laid on 15th December, 1873. At that ceremony a sum of £30.4.7d was raised and a tea and meeting raised £19.2.8d. The following year £726.14.1d was raised when the opening ceremony took place, reflecting its own story of sacrifice and devotion.

Dr Wearmouth was born at Oxhill and attended school there, leaving at aged 12 when he started work at Oxhill Pit. At 19 he ran away and joined the Northumberland Fusiliers and served in South Africa and West Indies. He returned with his regiment and while on furlough he was converted, wearing his army uniform in the little chapel at Oxhill. In 1914–1918 he served as Chaplain in France and Flanders. His academic achievements were BA, MA, BSc. Economics PhD degree. One of a notable series of books written by Dr Wearmouth is dedicated to the little chapel of Oxhill which sadly closed in 1978.

Pelton Lane Ends

Situated two miles west of Chester le Street, Pelton Lane Ends is a legacy of the mining era, one of the numerous self sufficient communities scattered around the area, linked by a network of mines and railways. The self sufficiency has gone, remaining are a collection of neat terraced houses, green fields, the schools, and most important the community spirit.

The village was mentioned in a publication in 1834 and was described as 'Pelton Lane that runs from west to east'.

At the eastern end of the Lane the infant and junior schools were opened in 1921 and were visited in 1928 by the Prince of Wales when he toured the area in the depression years following the 1926 miners' strike. At the western end of the Lane was built a most impressive Co-op, which was a notable landmark and feature of the area. The butchery department boasted its own abattoir; there was also a Co-op farm, stables, employees' houses and a social club for employees, providing sporting facilities. The Co-op was indeed a lifeline for most families in the area and customers came from miles around. During the 1960s this magnificent building was demolished and in the same period a modern piece of architecture was erected in the Lane, a large comprehensive school.

Nearby is Pelton Fell Park, opened in 1922. It has all the usual amenities and still serves the community today. The bandstand, however, was removed at a later date and placed in Chester le Street Park. Housed in the park is an impressive Cenotaph dedicated to the War Dead. In fact the entire Park was built and dedicated as a War Memorial. The cost of £6,000, an enormous sum at that time, was raised by subscription; all miners, railwaymen, and tradesmen in the area contributing weekly sums from their wages.

Among the network of railways in the area was an unusual self acting incline line, transporting coal from the Stanley area down to the Pelton area, eventually to be shipped out from Jarrow staithes and Tyne Dock.

Local transport was provided by Bobby Batemen – his brakes and carts were hired for all public and private outings, especially Sunday School trips. A very large rotund figure, he was never seen without a cigarette dangling from his lips, even when he drove the glass hearse which he also owned. Funerals were very spectacular when he drove the hearse, pulled by two black horses adorned with black ribbons and plumes. However, when he died in the early 1930s he was so large and fat his coffin had to be lifted through his bedroom window and put on a flat cart for his own funeral procession. Other characters were Little Tommy, the shopkeeper, a tiny man whose apron touched the floor. All the goods in the little dark shop were stored in large sacks and were weighed out by hand. One poor man, Mr Hankey, lost his home and raised his family in a hut on the allotments where his water supply was a fresh spring.

Near the western end of the Lane stands Pelton Holy Trinity Church, built in 1842. In 1928, the vicar at that time was very 'High Church' and wished to erect a statue in the church. This was neither wanted or approved by members of the church and after much trouble the case was referred to the Ecclesiastical Courts and the vicar lost his case. In revenge one Sunday morning, he excommunicated three members of the congregation. The sensational news travelled fast and by evensong the press were in position with cameras ready, but the vicar had conducted evensong earlier and the church doors were locked. This was his finale, for he was soon removed from Pelton.

In 1850 a stained glass window, known locally as the plague window was erected. This was to commemorate the preservation of the village when the plague swept the area with particular devastation in Chester le Street.

The Pelton Swine (a song published in 1834 origin obscure)

Who walks by night in Pelton Lane
May see a sight of fear
Five black swine that scurry by
And strange it is to hear
The jingling of their silver chains
as one by one they pass,
Three in the shadows of the dyke,
Two in the lonin'grass:
the patter of their cloven feet
As kirkward still they go,
An far behind is sometimes seen
A sixth one coming slow.
Right seldom do they come by day
and evil does it bode
To bride and bridegroom when they meet
The swine upon the road.
Five black swine in Pelton Lane
That runs from west to east
And still the sixth comes halting last
Barghest in shape of Beast. (Barghest was a sprite).
The swine come jingling down Pelton Lonin,
Five black swine and never an odd'en
Three i' the dyke and two i' the lonin,
Five black swine and never an odd'n.

Pittington & Littletown

The village of Pittington, made up of the original settlement – Low Pittington, High Pittington and Littletown. It is in the parish of Pittington which once extended to Durham in the west, Easington in the east, Houghton-le-Spring in the north and Kelloe in the south. The village nestles at the foot of Pittington Hill which is situated four miles south west of Durham. Its name derives from Pitt or Pytta, being the name of the chieftain and his clan, and Dun – the Hill. In the 12th century it was known as Pittingdune.

The parish church of St Lawrence, Hallgarth was originally built in 1050 and was at one time the only church between the river Wear and the North Sea. It was largely rebuilt in 1846–7 by Ignatious Bonomi. There is a rich variety of Norman and early English architecture with traces of Saxon edifice. Inside there are 12th century wall paintings depicting the consecration of St Cuthbert by Archbishop Theodore, and Cuthbert's vision at the table of the Abbess at Whitby.

Also in the church there is a tablet 'To the Memory of Mary Ann Westropp', who in her 18th year, on the eve of Sunday, 8th August 1830, was cruelly murdered. The beautiful young maid met her lover at Hallgarth Mill where the murder was committed. Her lover was executed at Durham on Monday, 28th February 1831. The ghost of Mary Ann is said to walk on Lady Peace Lane, and her cries were heard, borne on the wind, as far as High Pittington – but none claim to have seen her.

Hallgarth Manor House, once the home of the Priors is now Hallgarth Manor Hotel. The Manor House was approached by a beautiful avenue of ancient trees which are standing today, and looks toward the hill.

Pittington Hill is a limestone hill, once a thriving quarry, with superb views from the top. On a clear day you can see as far as Stanhope, Durham Cathedral and Penshaw Monument. In the summer there is an abundance of flora including violets, wild thyme, hairbell, grape hyacinth, common sorrel, braddon campion, wild strawberry, ladies bedstraw and many more. Quite rare now, but quite prolific in summer, are cowslip and purple orchids. During the Napoleonic war in 1804, a beacon was established on the hill to warn the inhabitants of any invasion attempts.

Littletown, in the past known as South Pittington, and later as Little Pittington, has been known as Littletown since 1613. Its township grew with the colliery, sunk in 1834 by Lord Durham, who also had the colliery school built in 1874. Very little of the original village remains today.

The Pittingtons and Littletown grew up through farming and limestone quarrying. Then came the era of the coal mining and the local railway. Little remains today of the industrial era of six pits in the area, owned by the Marquis of Londonderry, with its typical landscape of mining scars. This has all been reclaimed back to nature's own peaceful beauty which can be enjoyed by all, along the many fascinating walks around the village.

It is interesting to note that in 1801 the population stood at 220, increasing to 2,530 in 1851, its highest level. The latest figures available today total 1,616. Low Pittington 179, High Pittington 1,299 and Littletown 138.

Quaking Houses

The village of Quaking Houses was at one time called Old South Moor, but with the opening of the coalfields in 1839 new names came into being or were taken from old names connected with the area.

The following are facts and theories which could account for the origin of the name. Firstly there was a hill to the north west of the present village called Quaking Hill with Quaking House Cottages and Quaking House Farm nearby. In 1845 Wm Bell and Partners sank a pit on this hill which was originally called The New Shield Row, later the Quaking House Pit and finally the Charley Pit. Secondly legend has it that a Quaker once lived in one of the houses called The Barracks, built around the William Pit at the east end of the village. Mr Ned Herron, the colliery manager, lived in Bleak House which was built on or near quicksand. This patch of quicksand can be seen in the corner of the cricket field which is still in use. The house was later demolished and stones from Bleak House were used to build the high wall at the south end of the cricket field. And yet another theory is that an underground waggonway caused surface vibration therefore 'quaking the houses'.

Though small, the village has had some interesting people live there.

Fred Wade, a local historian and naturalist at one time lived in Third Street, and though he left school at a very early age wrote books about the area in which he lived. It is from his book on South Moor that most of this information has been researched. In the old days each village had women who were nurse and mid-wife. Mary Ann Gardiner who lived in Low Rows, Quaking Houses, was the lady villagers consulted in times of need, even to the pulling of teeth. She made a salve from an aromatic plant called Tansy, and when a product called Zambuk came on to the market it was said to smell like Mary Ann Gardiner's liniment.

To the south of Quaking Houses there is a moor called Morrow Edge. In 1933 a caravan colony had established itself in Morrow Edge Stone Quarry. Few of these caravans had wheels and most of them were nothing more than shanties or dugouts. There was no water, light or sanitation. After much debate the Council decided to evict the squatters and on October 25th, 1933, Mr J. Mackay, Bailiff of Consett, assembled a body of men to carry out the evictions. Several cases for damage were brought against the Council but all were dismissed. On March 8th, 1939, James R. Rainbow, retired hack master sued the Council for damages in regard to the destruction of one caravan and the removal of five others from his land known as Rainbow's Yard. He won his case and was awarded £560 damages.

From 1839 pits were sunk in the area which meant work for people, and with people came houses, schools, churches, shops and inns. Within the confines of approximately one square mile Quaking Houses had three schools. The National, built in Wagtail Lane in 1847, Old South Moor built in 1889, and the South Moor Mixed School built in January 1901 to serve both Old and New South Moor. There were three pits, the William 1839, the Charley which eventually became the brickworks, sunk in 1845, and the Hedley, sunk in 1885. A Wesleyan Church was built in 1858. There were three inns: The Smiths, The Oak and The Stag on the same side of the road and all within a space of 100 yards plus a brewery and a number of shops. There was still room for two farms, a plantation and a moor.

The pits are now closed and modern day occupations are found in towns and cities. There have been changes in the village since it was first founded. The old houses have been renovated and most are still standing today.

When a colliery village comes into being, with families brought together through the need for work, within a few generations a close bond is forged, and if the village still stands after the reason for its formation has disappeared, the roots are still there. How long this will last only time will tell.

Redworth

The village of Redworth is situated one mile north of Heighington and five miles south south-east of Bishop Auckland. The earliest records of Redworth are in the Boldon Book in 1183.

In the early 20th century most of the cottages in the village were the properties of the Surtees family, who lived in Redworth Hall; which is now the well known Redworth Hall Hotel and Health Club.

The only water for the village was the village pump from which residents carried in their buckets their daily supply of water. There was no electricity in the village. There were two public house, The Surtees Arms and The Pack Horse Inn.

The Wesleyan chapel dated 1878 is now the village hall and is the venue for monthly WI meetings.

The cottages were sold by the Surtees family to the residents and others for as little as £50 and now the village has had new houses and bungalows built it has doubled in size and is still a very attractive and desirable place to live.

The old joiners shop has been transformed into a lovely stonebuilt home, the old post office is now the home of the Smith family, and the old blacksmiths shop is now the home of the Whitehead family.

The late Peggy Hutchinson, authoress of many cookery and winemaking books lived for a number of years in the village.

We now have water on tap, electricity, gas, telephone, and a good bus service; but, no shops, no pubs and no post office (except a postal collection box).

Romaldkirk

'Rumold Church
Rum Old Steeple
Rumold Parish
Rum Old People'

Romaldkirk derives its name from a 10th century Saxon church dedicated to a little known Saint Romald. Situated on a road which follows the river Tees – roughly halfway between Barnard Castle and Middleton-in-Teesdale. It is a village of 100 houses and 150 inhabitants, looking very much the same since the stone cottages were built in the Middle Ages around three village greens. On High Green there sits a village pump, also one on Low Green – both in use until 1936. Middle Green has stocks which have been preserved for posterity. Just to the north is a stream called Beerbeck (a combination of Saxon and Norwegian, both beer and beck meaning stream). One old landmark is the Pound which is still there by the beck. Four walls made a small enclosure into which straying animals were put by the Pindar who charged a fine of 1d for a horse, ½d for a beast or sheep. In 1693 William Hutchinson bequeathed money for six Almshouses to be built overlooking Beerbeck.

Qualification of occupancy was being of Protestant religion, attending Church on Sundays, generally over 60 years of age and had to be in their houses by 9pm in summer and 7pm in winter. The Almshouses, now known as Hutchinson Terrace, outwardly look the same but have been made into three comfortable homes for the elderly. In the old days there was a village nurse and also our own policeman on the beat. There were at one time five Inns and a Brewery all within a short distance of one another. Only two now remain, the Kirk and the Rose and Crown. There were also three general shops, a drapers, a cottage where the owner displayed home made sticks and crooks and of course there was a blacksmith shop. In recent years only one general dealer/post office remained but that is now closed. The Kirk Inn has taken over the post office, so for stamps, pensions etc. it means a visit to the pub. The Rose and Crown was an old coaching inn with a mounting block but the latter has been removed to make a window for a new dining room. On the forecourt the paving stones are an unusual memorial to Queen Victoria giving the initials of Her Majesty and the dates of her reign. Opposite to the Rose and Crown we are fortunate to have a large village hall known as the Reading Room and the dedication on the doorway lintel is to Edward VII. This has a full sized snooker table upstairs and the hall itself is well used by WI, aerobic classes, yoga, film shows etc. Every August a Summer Fair is held. A marquee is erected on Low Green for Tombola and an assortment of other stalls. Children's races and other activities are held in the open air and teas are available in the Reading Room. A far cry from fairs of old when gipsies brought horses, cows and sheep. Stalls were outside the Rose and Crown selling all kinds of goods including a popular toffee called 'cure all'. Horses on leading reins ran up and down the road. The fair was stopped in 1930 due to riotous behaviour. Transport in the early days was horseback, a carriage and trap and the carriers cart until 1876 when a single line railway ran from Barnard Castle to Middleton-in-Teesdale. This is no longer in operation – closed 28 November 1964 – motorised transport has taken over. A reminder of the railway is the Station now converted into a house with the original signal outside as a feature. The village school was flourishing in the 1900s and had a very good choir which was chosen by the BBC to broadcast with Joyce Bainbridge singing the solos. This was a great honour as they were chosen out of all of Teesdale. From a school of 90 pupils it closed in 1930 with 6, but in 1939 it was opened again for evacuees. The building is still in good condition and is used weekly as a kindergarten. All older children now go by bus to a school in a neighbouring village.

There is much history in this area of the marauding Scots and in 1070 Malcolm King of the Scots laid the entire district waste including the original Saxon Church. The building of the present St Romald's Church was started in 1150 and added to 1280 and later still 1360–70. In the north transept is an effigy of Sir Hugh Fitz Henry showing armour of Edward I period in outstanding detail. The Fitz Hugh family had the patronage of the living in medieval times. The present patron is Lord Strathmore. It is rather remarkable that in a place as small as Romaldkirk three of our rectors became Bishops. William Knight, Bishop of Bath and Wells 1541, Owen Oglethorpe who crowned Elizabeth I was made Bishop of Carlisle 1557 and Richard Barnes Bishop of Carlisle in 1570. One rector in 1808 was Reginald Bligh, a relative of Bligh of the *Bounty*. Today we are fortunate to have a resident rector living in the Rectory near the Church. Besides St Romald's he is in charge of two other parishes. One tradition is still carried out today at a wedding. The church gates are tied and the bridegroom throws money to the other side for them to be opened.

The great plague struck Romaldkirk in 1644 when one third of the population was completely wiped out, but the memory of one outstanding character remains. Grace Scott who fled from the village and built herself a hut of mud and turf high up on the moor where she lived until all danger was past. The hut is no longer there but a stone farmstead was built in its place and is still known as Gracies Cottage.

Today there is still a working dairy farm at the bottom of the village, also a smallholding rearing llamas. Today's inhabitants have very different occupations such as local government officers, a prison officer, a potato merchant, a plastic surgeon, teachers, an artist, an owner of a factory making motor cycle leathers and a mixture of other professional people who commute to nearby towns. There are also quite a few retired people pleased to live in an area of outstanding natural beauty. The church is known as the Cathedral of the Dale and the village is mentioned in the Domesday Book.

Rookhope

The quiet Weardale village of Rookhope, 1,100 feet above sea level, surrounded by hills and moorland, is situated six miles south of the very centre of Great Britain. It has a population of about 300. The Prince Bishops hunted here and deer can still be spotted in woodland on the edge of the village. In the 16th century the villagers had to defend their homes and stock from the Moss Troopers. Details of the raid are recounted in an old ballad called the *Rookhope Ryde* composed in 1572. There are 17 verses which tell how the raiders were driven off with heavy losses.

Rookhope was once a thriving, working lead mining village with a washing plant, smelt mill and railway. Miners travelled from outlying districts, some often walking long distances, bringing with them sufficient food to last a week and living in the Miners' lodging house, known as the 'shop'. When the lead mine was no longer viable it had to close, but fluorspar is extracted further along the valley which is valuable to the steel industry. This provides a certain amount of employment but the majority of people now have to travel outside the area. Many original inhabitants have settled in other parts of the country and even abroad. Houses which became vacant are often bought by 'incomers' seeking a quieter life.

The village boasts a thriving Plant Nurseries which attracts many visitors from all over the country. The owners of Weardale Knitwear live in Rookhope and have created original designs depicting the rural life of the area.

Because of the prosperity from the mining industry there were once 8 shops, but after its decline only the post office/store remains open.

There was a Primitive Chapel (now a dwelling house), a Wesleyan Chapel which is still used, and a Church which, because of dampness in its original location near the burn, was rebuilt on the hill where services are still held. A former vicar, the Rev Arthur W. Officer, was one of the longest-serving vicars in Britain, taking services even after he became blind. He came in 1919 and died at the age of 92 after a ministry of 53 years in Rookhope.

There is still a Primary and Junior School but Senior pupils travel by bus to Wolsingham.

The villagers have always been very united in their fight for facilities to enhance their lives. In 1960 a Village Hall was opened which was built partly by public subscription following extensive money-raising events. It is used for various activities including the meetings of the WI now in its 70th year. Another combined effort resulted in the erection of a TV Relay system when the men of the village voluntarily worked with a contractor to provide this service.

In the past there were two brass bands and one jazz band, but now sadly gone. The Mens' Institute and Reading Rooms have disappeared but the WI continues.

It is recounted that each year the young men of the village used to bring all the farmers' gates down into the centre of the village to the Weighbridge on New Year's Eve. On New Year's Day all the farmers had to collect them. Again, traditionally, some of the braver schoolchildren took unofficial holiday, saying:

> 29th May – Royal Oak Day
> If you don't give us holiday
> We'll all run away.

But they had to face the music the following day!

After lapsing for many years the Carnival was revived in 1977 and has continued ever since providing a very colourful and entertaining day in June.

1,200 ft underground is a huge block of hot granite which could yield hot springs. However after investigative boring, the discovery of an obstruction which would be too costly to remove, meant the project had to be abandoned.

When there is sufficient snow, skiing can take place on the slopes. The area was once earmarked for a ski village. Also, because of its open location, it was suggested for a wind farm. Eventually neither of these projects was selected, so the flora and fauna remain undisturbed, left to be admired by the hikers who pass through on the Weardale Way.

Rushyford

The postal district of Rushyford covers a series of hamlets covered by the old Windlestone estate. These hamlets are groups of cottages built for estate workers and estate farms together with areas now townships in themselves like Newton Aycliffe, Woodham and Chilton. The main hamlet which is what we now consider the village of Rushyford was built round the ford over the Rushyford Beck or the Black Beck which flows into the river Skerne near Preston-on-Skerne. It also marks the crossing of the old London to Edinburgh road – the old stage-coach road.

Rushyford's first claim to notoriety came in 1317. In the autumn of that year Lewis Beaumont, a cousin of Queen Isabella of Angouleme, who had been nominated Bishop of Durham was travelling north for his enthronement. He was accompanied by his brother, two cardinals and a retinue of servants. As they came to the gloomy stream at Rushyford the party was set upon by a band of robbers led by Gilbert Middleton. Lewis Beaumont was carried off to Mitford Castle and held to ransom. After being robbed the rest of the travellers were allowed to continue on their way, but Beaumont was held prisoner until the ransom demanded was paid.

Until the road alterations in 1931 a tablet let into the bridge facing the Eden Arms Hotel recorded the incident.

By 1538 land was given to the Eden family at Windlestone and by 1588 John Maison, or Eden, the natural son of John Eden of Windlestone had founded the dynasty. His son Robert succeeded to the property at the time of the Civil Wars, most of the local land-owners of that time being Royalist. At the end of 1643 John Eden, the young son of Robert was granted a commission by Charles I to raise a regiment over which he was to become Colonel (the original document bearing the commission was kept at Windlestone until the estate was sold in 1936).

After the defeat of the King, Robert Eden was fined approximately ⅙ the annual value of the estate. It has been said that in order to pay his fine much of the forest of Oaks at Windlestone were cut down and sold. At the same time the forest at Woodham was supposedly cut down on an order from Cromwell so as to make the roads passable for his army and equipment. Skirmishes between the two armies took place at Woodham Moor. After the Restoration of the Monarchy in 1660 Robert Eden was one of 687 gentlemen to be made a Knight of the Royal Oak.

In 1675 another Robert succeeded to the Windlestone Estate and it was he who was created a Baronet.

During the 18th century however, the point marked on maps as Rushyford probably grew from just a road junction to a hamlet. The stage-coach became the mode of transport and the inn at Rushyford was the changing place for horses. The site of the inn appears to have been moved more than once. At that time, it is believed to have been the last of the block of houses opposite the Eden Arms. When one owner of the 1950s to 1960s had mounting stones removed from his front garden and when the bridge over the beck was removed many horseshoes were removed from the water.

Successive generations of the Eden family owned the Windlestone Estate and lived in the Manor House. In 1873 Sir William took over at his father's death. Sir William was a very colourful character, a good landlord but rather a tyrant. He did carry out improvements to the Hall, its grounds and its game preserves, and planted many acres of trees. He also improved the tenant-farmers' holdings.

Mel Suppers or Harvest Home Suppers were held on the estate up to about 1887 when the last one was held in the granary at the Home Farm. One man at the party had had his best clothes stored away in pepper and the subsequent sneezing caused great merriment and was never forgotten.

In the early 20th century Lady Eden arranged for a wagon to take the estate servants to the church of her preference either to St Andrews, Kirk Merrington or to Coundon. Every Christmas all the children of the Windlestone Estate were invited to the Hall for a great Christmas treat.

They were taken into the Hall and had tea and crackers. They would go along a wide corridor before passing through a green baize door into the front part of the house with the wide staircase, the oak panels and the large portraits on the walls, to where the large Christmas tree stood with brightly-lit candles and decorations and a fairy doll at the top. Parcels for the children were piled around the foot of the tree and Lady Eden would call out the name of each child who would go forward to receive a parcel which the girls acknowledged with a curtsey. On other occasions Lady Eden visited the school at Rushyford to leave presents.

In the summer of each year there was a trip to the seaside. In the morning carts from Home Farm would take the children to the station and in the evening bring them back again.

Lady Eden is still thought of as the Lady Bountiful of the village as she was always prepared to help when she heard of villagers in trouble. Every Sunday the governess from the Hall held a Sunday School class in the Mausoleum Chapel. The children had to wait outside the high stone wall until she came along to unlock the little wooden gate in the wall which is still there.

When the Eden family first bought cars they had them painted yellow with black lines and wheels. The first car that stopped at Rushyford pulled into the village at the same time as the travelling draper was calling there and the draper's horse was so badly frightened by the sight and sound of the strange vehicle that it had to be stabled at the inn overnight in the cobbled courtyard and the draper walked home.

During the First World War, Windlestone Hall was used as a hospital for wounded army men. About this time in 1915 Sir William died and was buried – not in the mausoleum but by his special request in the grounds of the estate.

The death of Sir William and the tragic loss of two of his sons in a period of less than two years put a great strain on the estate by way of taxes and death duties and in 1936 Sir Timothy was compelled to sell the estate. The whole estate of some 4,000 acres was sold by auction in November, 1936.

There was the central block of buildings in Rushyford which included the Manor House with its stabling and loose boxes, the Eden Arms and between these two were two cottages. At the back of these buildings were the Rushyford Institute and Reading Room and the Rookery House.

The block of houses on the other side of the road included the Joiner's shop and smithy and the post office. These have all closed and the smithy altered and renovated as part of the adjacent cottage. The post office has also now closed.

The various cottages, Well cottages, Mill cottages, etc, were mostly occupied by servants to the Eden family and Estate workers. Sir Timothy said that these had to be retained by the tenants on a rent-free basis for life. If they wished they could buy the houses, Sir Timothy lending many of them money for this purpose. He also helped tenant-farmers on the estate with money with which to buy their farms.

The whole of the block which included the Eden Arms is now a luxury hotel. All of the trees were cut down to open up the front of the hotel and the road junction has been altered in an effort to improve road safety.

Windlestone Hall was used for a while by the Wayfarers' Benevolent Association but when the Second World War broke out it was used as a camp for German prisoners-of-war and later as a home for displaced persons from the Baltic. During this time a great deal of damage was done to the hall grounds – the mausoleum being so vandalised and raided for lead that when a coffin was found opened it had to be demolished.

The Hall was finally bought by Durham County Council and opened as a Residential School for Delicate Children in July, 1958. It is now a School for Children with Behavioural and Emotional Difficulties. The Hall and its grounds have been greatly altered and modernised.

Rushyford with its closely-knit links with the Eden family and its fortunes has roots which go deep down into the agricultural rural existence of four or five centuries ago. Those families still in existence in the area must be very proud of their heritage.

In some ways while we welcome progress we face a new modern generation with our new housing estates. Let's hope that with this new generation we can become as closely knit as our predecessors.

Sacriston

Do good things exist in the North-East of England? Most certainly they do! Sacriston Village for one thing, its people past and present, and its celebrities.

Sacriston, a pleasant village, lies three miles north-west of Durham City. When coal was located, two coal shafts were sunk, Sacriston and

Witton. Rows of colliery houses were built. Miners from Cornwall and Staffordshire were brought to increase production – hence four streets, now demolished, were called the Staffordshire Rows. The colliery was well located at the bottom of the village, not obvious or intrusive, being surrounded by country and a variety of trees.

The village is now changed, since there is no colliery. Several private housing estates, catering for all age groups, provide a wider community spirit. The council have built welcome new accommodation in the form of one and two bedroomed bungalows. They were enterprising too, in building two Units, housing 50 Senior Citizens, in comfortable warden controlled flats providing sheltered accommodation.

The main road from Stanley to Durham is crossed by the Chester-le-Street road leading inland to the country, controlled by traffic lights.

On a well chosen plot near the crossroads is part of the colliery winding-wheel, with a plaque commemorating the dangerous work done by brave miners in past years.

Half-way up the main street is the previous Miners' Institute, converted into a well-appointed Community Centre, complete with clock tower. The Centre caters for all age groups, including a happy playgroup, and is used each day.

Sacriston children are well provided for. Outside the Community Centre is a 'Zebra' crossing, where Primary School children are often seen crossing, in the safe hands of their teachers, en-route to the village swimming baths. Primary School children now use the old 'County' schools, with adequate space to include a small nursery school. A large comprehensive school 'Fyndoune' enjoys an excellent position at the top of Findon Hill, overlooking Durham City and Durham Cathedral on its glorious site.

The parish church of St Peter and the Roman Catholic St Bede's Church and school are almost side by side. There is St John's Methodist Church and a Salvation Army Citadel.

A flourishing men's meeting, non-political and non-religious, continues year after year, a cross section of the population.

Cricket has always been a popular sport in Sacriston. The level area behind the Community Centre makes cricket, bowls, tennis and football possible. Bobby Robson, the former manager of the English football team, was born in Sacriston.

Senior Citizens find relaxation in an 'Over-60s' Club, held in the Working Men's Club, and in a Pensioners' Association in the Community Centre. There is a Ladies Club and of course the WI, meeting in the Community Centre.

The popular actress, Wendy Craig, was also born in Sacriston. Her grandmother was once headmistress of the infants' School, and lived to a great age.

We hope you have found in this account of our village that Sacriston has always had, and does have, some capable, friendly and interesting people. A very good thing!

Sadberge

Sadberge is a pleasant village of some 600 inhabitants situated on a hill surrounded by farmland, a comfortable distance from the busy A66 Darlington to Stockton road which has helped to divert through traffic away from the village.

Despite new development, Sadberge retains its village character with Church, houses, pubs and shop clustered round the village green. The children no longer attend the old village school which is now a busy village hall; their new school is still within the village boundary. A peaceful picture, far removed from the days when the area was a Roman encamped, standing on the road, which ran south, crossing the river Tees at Pounteys Bridge in nearby Middleton St George to York and beyond and to the north, possibly terminating at the river Tyne.

Later in medieval times it became an area of considerable importance with its own Assize Court and Sheriffs. The Three Tuns pub was once the local court and the cells are now the pub cellars.

In 1189, in Norman times, the Wapentake of Sadberge was purchased by Bishop Pudsey from King Richard the First, with the Earldom of Northumberland, for life.

A reference to its attachment to the Crown can be seen on the glacier Boulder Stone on the village green, commemorating the jubilee of Queen Victoria in 1887.

The original Saxon church was demolished in 1825 by a Darlington builder for the sum of £10 and the present church was then built nearby in 1831 retaining two pre-reformation bells and two small carved figures from the ancient church.

The Sadberge Methodist Chapel in Chapel Row built in 1869 at a cost of £250 stood the test of time but was reluctantly closed in June 1991 after one hundred and twenty two years of service to the community.

Little remains of the past glories of Sadberge save its Saxon name – The Hill of Pleas – possibly so called as taxes were collected here in Saxon times and the collectors would no doubt have listened to the pleas from those being heavily taxed, a feeling which lives on some 800 years later!

St Helen Auckland

The ancient church of St Helen Auckland dates from 1150 but many additions have been made over the years.

There are many detailed descriptions of the wonderful windows, arches, brasses and carvings. The parvis above the porch providing accommodation for visiting Priests is rare, and some of the original steps to it can be seen inside the church. The door is very old and some of the oak pews are Jacobean. The ancient belltower has an inscription in latin – 'St Helen – pray for us'.

Famous names associated with St Helen Auckland are Cuthbert Carr, Ralph Eden and an emotive entry in the register on Feb 4th 1647 recording the fact that King Charles I stayed at an inn in Bishop Auckland while being conveyed as a prisoner on his way to execution in London.

A very fine tower on Brusselton Hill was the landmark for St Helen Auckland. It was an octagonal building approached by a long flight of steps. The rococo decor at the Hall was echoed here and the views from here scan many miles to the sea, the Cleveland Hills, the Pennines and Durham Cathedral.

It was known locally as Brusselton Folly and had a permanent watchman named as 'Folly Frank'. One of the fields around the hill was the 'Chopping Axe' field due to its shape. It was here that families congregated on feast days; spending happy hours rolling their pace eggs – (hard boiled and dyed) having picnics, arranging games and races for the children, with refreshments of tea, home made ginger beer and tonic being served from the Folly. Then the local Silver Band entertained the populace. Sadly the Folly crumbled over the years and as fire gutted it in the 1930s, it must have been removed as unsafe. Coal was now the main industry of the district and Brusselton Pit was one of many in the area. Again local names used were not the feminine ones listed such as Catherine and Emma, but only nicknames like Broken Balk and Town End etc. Many of the seams were named and rhymed off by an aged resident, Mr W Longstaff, who worked in most of these pits as a mining engineer and lived to the grand old age of 95.

A handsome building with a varied history is St Helen's Hall. It began modestly as a three storey house built around 1610. The panelling in this position is still in good order. There was a beautiful staircase, which has recently been removed by the Eden family. A secret room was found during alterations with no door or windows. Little is documented about the many owners but famous names included are the Edens, the Daltons, Carrs and Milbanks and many more. The House is described as a 'Stateman's House' but when the Georgian wing was added with its tasteful Palladian influence the house became 'grand'.

Another owner was the M.P. Sir Joseph Pease who was responsible for opening a reading-cum-pool room for the miners.

Several tenancies later the latest occupier is Mr William Whitfield and the Hall shows a well tended appearance. Over the years several legends abounded such as the tunnel, said to lead to the folly but never proven though one old resident once told of being put down a short flight of steps in the dark where said tunnel had been bricked up. This was her punishment for misdeeds. Another story has the tunnel leading to the church, but nothing has ever come to light. Once a year there are loud noises of a horse drawn carriage or coach being driven in the stable area of St Helens Hall. That is the only record of a ghost story so far.

Houses built for the miners had a slate set in the wall near the front door and this was used to write the time he needed the 'knocker up' to know when to tap on his bedroom window with the long pole he carried for this purpose.

Not all the miners' time was spent underground. He had his fresh air pursuits, growing vegetables and enormous leeks to enter in the annual shows, this was a very competitive occupation and everyone had their own growing secrets. Whippets and greyhounds were trained for racing, lurchers used for hunting rabbits, quoits were played and public houses catered for these with special alleys. Miners were paid fortnightly and the Saturday between known as Baff Saturday – or going begging. There was a quotation for this: 'The Baff week is o'er – no repining, Pay Saturday's swift on the wing!' When the coal seams petered out due to strata faults and flooding, wage disputes and the General Strike caused great poverty and St Helens became a distress area. Soup kitchens were set up in the Workmen's Institute which was the pool and reading room provided by Pease and Partners, Eton College sponsored the area with food parcels and helping the unemployed. The women of the village used their skills in needlework, crochet, quilting, patchwork and most popular of all the 'clippy' mats. These were made from old jackets and coats cut into small strips and worked into hessian. The designs were original and a lot of work went into them. Huge frames were set up and all the family could work at them.

The boys from Eton College were guests at Raby Castle and came for chats to the miners and football matches were arranged.

There are photographs of all this and the Eton Hall that was sponsored by the Southern Counties was built with many of the unemployed doing the work. Then courses were arranged and the people could learn trades such as repairing furniture, shoes and boots and many other trades.

A sampler worked by an ancestor of a local farming family is on loan to Bowes Museum. The design includes the family pets, a tree and the verse as follows:

'On the tree of life eternal,
Oh let all our hopes be laid
This alone forever vernal
Bears a leaf that will not fade.'

There was a communal bakery as the houses once used as barracks had no amenities. Water was carried on wooden yokes, and wash day was also a communal affair. An outsize weighted mangle was installed in the old bakery and used also for grinding meal. Each week a piece of dough was kept and put in the next batch of bread thus producing Sour Leaven Bread, made into flat cakes or wheels.

Beamish Museum also houses relics from St Helen Auckland Barn; machinery for working grinding wheels.

Half a mile down the road to Bishop Auckland is Tindale Crescent near to Fieldon's Bridge. Here there was a thriving Methodist Chapel and a school for infants, prior to moving on to the Junior School now near St Helen's Vicarage, and once on the site of the Roman Catholic Church a hospital was opened at Tindale Crescent for infectious diseases at a cost of £8000.

Precious buildings and relics have gone over the years. The barracks behind St Helen's Hall was made into a dwelling house, a beautiful old house nearby was demolished and a brand new nursing home stands in its stead. The old ovens and horse shoe stonewall, first built to keep cattle from straying, stocks once on a green in front of the Hall, and other relics have long gone.

Now built over the green fields are streets of council houses and sadly little of the village atmosphere remains, except for thriving organisations such as guides, scouts, Mothers Union, Neighbourhood Centre Clubs, Women's Institute and Community Centre activities.

A trading estate, a Cash & Carry and a motel have completely changed St Helen Auckland from a sleepy backwater to a mainstream of activity.

St John's Chapel

St John's Chapel takes its name from the church, built in 1465, around which it grew. There were previous forest settlements at Harthopeburn and Burnfoot, which are now part of the village. There is record of lead mining at Harthope in 1425 and in 1438 a group of miners paid 40/- rent for a mine there and had grazing for 30 pack animals used for the transport of lead ore. These miners lived at 'the place later known as St John's Chapel'. By 1752 this church, built as a chapel of ease attached to the church at Stanhope, was too small for a community which had grown with the clearing of the forest, the establishment of farmsteads and, more dramatically, with the development of lead and ironstone mining.

The second church was built by Sir Walter Blackett, lessee of the lead mines, with a legacy of £50 from Dr Hartwell, rector of Stanhope. It is Georgian in style with windows, apart from those with stained glass, oddly domestic. The chancel was added in 1881.

In 1951 a tablet in the church was unveiled in memory of William Morley Egglestone, 'Antiquary, Historian and Public Servant'. Born at St John's Chapel in 1838 he worked in the lead mines, possibly from the age of eight, until his early twenties, when he opened a shop in the

Market Place at St John's Chapel. A stationer and newsagent, he also sold a variety of goods ranging from violins to mouse traps. With a wide range of interests – local and natural history, folk lore, dialect, geology – and an inborn facility with words, fostered by reading, he began writing newspaper articles and, having set up his own printing press, published some of these as pamphlets. He had a keen sense of humour and wrote comical tales, including the popular adventures of Betty Podkins.

In 1874 Egglestone obtained the post of Inspector of Nuisances for the parishes of Stanhope, Wolsingham, Hunstanworth and Edmundbyers and moved from St John's Chapel to Stanhope. His writing continued but he also studied diligently all subjects connected with his new appointment and gained several first class certificates. Valuable as was his work in providing water supplies and sewerage to Weardale villages, he is best remembered for his writings, sought for and treasured by students of local history.

The Rev James Whitehead Pattison was vicar of St John's Chapel from 1906 until his death in 1936. He was a keen photographer and his album of prints and slides were given to Bowes Museum by his daughter. His photographs of children and agricultural workers are delightful pictures and interesting social documents. Although a village, St John's Chapel boasts a Town Hall, built in 1866 on the village green and rebuilt after a fire in 1952. The memorial in front of the hall lists the names of those who fell in the First and Second World Wars and records the death of seven airmen whose plane crashed at Greenlaws in 1943. Near the Town Hall is the smaller Barrington Hall, built as a school in 1819 and now used for various village functions. The present junior school, built in 1877 and extended twice in the last thirty years, is at Burnfoot, beyond the play park that was once the village pinfold. A Primitive Methodist Chapel was built in 1852 on the site that is now the entrance to the caravan park and taken down in 1960 after the Union of the Methodist Churches. The Wesleyan Chapel, built in 1869, stands half-way up Hood Street.

Poaching grouse on the moors was looked upon as a right by lead miners but frowned upon by the authorities. In 1818, in a determined attempt to apprehend the poachers, a party of men from Bishop Auckland and another from Darlington joined forces at Wolsingham and marched up to St John's Chapel where they were met by the Bishop's gamekeeper and the landlord of the Black Bull (now the Co-operative

Store). Charles and Anthony Siddle, who lived in a cottage behind the Kings Head, attempted to escape over the roof but, the weather being frosty, slipped and fell and were taken prisoner. Other poachers had been warned and were not to be found so the two prisoners were taken to Stanhope by cart. A body of poachers followed, a bloody fight ensued known as 'The Battle of Stanhope', the Siddles were freed and the poachers returned home in triumph. As the ballad says:

> 'The Miners of Weardale are all valiant men.
> They will fight till they die for the Bonny Moor Hen.'

In 1820 the Weardale Park and Forest Association for the Prosecution of Felons was founded for the protection of the persons and property of the members and the bringing of criminals to justice.

The crimes recorded range from the stealing of the Rev Green's linen to the savage assault by three drunken men on an innkeeper and his wife. The society is now a purely social affair, meeting once a year at the King's Arms for dinner with a guest speaker, generally someone connected with the law. Any members arriving after 6 pm by the church clock are fined half a crown. The committee, elected every year, is chosen by lot from members who reside in the Park or Forest.

The Weardale Agricultural Show has been held in the Glebe Field since 1868. Here, on the last Saturday in August, farmers display their livestock and crafts, cookery and photographs are also shown and judged. At the eastern end of the village is the Mart, founded in 1895 and the main centre for Swaledale sheep in County Durham. Sales of sheep and cattle are held in the autumn and it is only then and at Show time that St John's Chapel, becomes the busy, bustling place it was when lead mining was at its height.

Satley

Satley is an attractive small village, surrounded by farmland, lying astride the road midway between Lanchester and Tow Law.

The focus of the village is the stone-built church, dedicated to St Cuthbert. This sturdy building has a low, square bell-tower housing steps leading up to the western gallery. Two beautifully carved grave covers, of former priests of Satley, are built into the west wall of the

St Cuthbert's Church, Satley

nave. They were saved from the ruins of an earlier building when the present church was restored in 1870. The plane trees around the churchyard were planted in 1775.

The house by the churchyard gate was built as a school in 1816, at the cost of £120. It replaced Satley's original school which was housed in two thatched cottages, dating from 1790, and standing in a field close to Steeley Farm (they were demolished in 1867.) This new school was in use until 1846, when it too was replaced by a larger one, built at the other side of the churchyard gate, which served Satley for over 100 years. It was closed in 1965 to make way for a new modern building, built in a field behind the houses in Glebeside. This, however, only served until 1979 when it also closed and from that date the children of Satley have been taken by bus to schools in Tow Law or Wolsingham.

When it was closed as a school in 1965, the building by the churchyard gate became the Parish Hall and is now the venue for most of the activities of the parish, which includes the villages of Cornsay and Hedleyhope, the hamlets of Browney Bank, East and West Butsfield, Broomshields and Prospect along with numerous surrounding farms.

The village boasts two public houses – the Royal Oak, built in 1865, and the larger, much modernised Punch Bowl.

Unfortunately the village shop-cum-post-office has now closed. Post Office facilities are available on four mornings per week, at a house in the village, but for general shopping, people without cars have to rely on a very infrequent bus service.

Satley once had its own cobbler, blacksmith and miller. Sadly all have now gone, although the mill still stands as a testimony to what once was. The vicarage, too, is now a private house, – the Parish having been amalgamated with that of Tow Law – and there is no longer a resident policeman in the village.

Notwithstanding these changes, Satley is still very much alive – a friendly, thriving village at the centre of a farming community.

Satley's history goes back to the period before Christianity. Flint spear-heads and arrows of Neolithic times have been unearthed, and also two Ancient British graves – one at Satley Grange, and the other, containing human remains, and also burial urns filled with food, was found in 1888 between East and West Butsfield.

The name Satley is Anglo Saxon and means 'an enclosed meadow by the wayside' and the road through the village originated as a track from Lanchester Roman Camp to Weardale. Several Roman coins have been found in the village; also coins of the reign of King Egbert and King Alfred.

Built into the wall of a barn, (originally the farm house) at Steeley Burn Farm is the gravestone of Thomas Raw, of Wharnley Burn, near Castleside. He was one of the last of the fearless, but lawless mosstroopers, who stole cattle, burning farms and terrorising the people along the Scottish borders. He died in 1714 and his inscribed tombstone was moved from Wharnley Burn to Satley in 1886.

Opposite the Parish Hall are two semi-detached cottages – originally almshouses, donated to the poor of Satley by a Miss Margaret Moscrop in memory of her fiance, Rev George Ellam, who was killed in a motor cycle accident in 1905, 27 days after becoming the vicar of Satley.

Another famous name connected with Satley is that of Lieut. R. A. Warneford, remembered as the first man to shoot down a German

Zeppelin single-handed in 1915. This daring feat earned him the VC. Lieut. Warneford was the nephew of Rev Warneford, Vicar of Satley.

Much of this knowledge of the village was amassed by Thomas William Fawcett, the famous soldier, traveller and historian – secretary of the Durham Historical Society for many years, who retired to Satley and died there in 1942 – in the village with which his family had been connected since 1596.

Sedgefield

Sedgefield occupies a low hill of gravel in pleasant countryside eleven miles south east of the city of Durham on the A177 road to Teesside. Sedgefield's market charter dates back from 1312 and the town itself goes back to the tenth century and was occupied by the Normans.

In the 10th and 11th centuries it was known as 'Ceddesfeld', and in the 12th and 13th centuries as 'Seggefeld' or 'Segesfeld'. One of these ancient names lives on in the name of Ceddesfeld Hall, a large building which was previously the rectory but now houses the thriving Sedgefield Community Association. The living was obviously an important one for the incumbents often moved on to higher office, the 18th century producing four subsequent bishops.

St Edmund's church dates from the 13th century and has an impressive tower added in the 15th century by Robert Rodes; it stands 90 ft high and is crowned by octagonal turrets with battlements and pinnacles.

The curfew bell used to be tolled from the church tower; it was rung at 8.00pm in the winter and 9.00pm in the summer. After the curfew the bell is tolled an appropriate number of times to signify the date.

Sedgefield's most famous legend of the Pickled Parson dates back to the late 18th century. The story goes that the parson died just before the tithes were due to be paid, and his wife, wanting to ensure safe receipt of these, pickled her husband's body in brine so that no-one should know of his death; she then positioned his body in a window for his parishioners to see.

The present Roman Catholic Church was built in the 1930s, and was the first one in the world to be dedicated to St John Fisher.

Sedgefield is one of the few places where the ancient Shrove Tuesday football game is still played, using a mini-football slightly bigger than a cricket ball. The game starts at one o'clock with the ball being passed through the bull-ring thrice, whereupon the townsfolk and the country folk contend for it. The ball must be alleyed before six o'clock.

During previous centuries Sedgefield was an important coaching centre. Since Sedgefield stood on the Turnpike Road from Durham to Stockton, coaches stopped here to set down and pick up passengers and to change horses. The coaching inn was the Hardwick Arms.

Nowadays it is well-known for its racecourse which is the only one in County Durham. Sedgefield came into prominence in the equestrian world in 1804, as it was the headquarters of the famous Lambton Hunt.

There was a public bakehouse on the site where the library now stands, and here the poor were given bread free at week-ends. A sale of geese was held every year, the birds being brought from Ireland with their feet padded with tar for travelling.

Shadforth

Shadforth parish lies four miles east of Durham City and includes the village of Ludworth and part of Sherburn Hill. Shadforth itself nestles in the valley of Shadforth Beck and is a quiet settlement with mainly white and grey houses lining a long, narrow green. The 19th century church of St Cuthbert stands on rising ground on the opposite side of the beck, near the small council housing estate and a few private houses in front of the church.

A mile upstream from the village stands the gaunt ruin of Ludworth Tower, which guards the approach to the tiny 19th century mining village of Ludworth. The mine closed several years ago, and all that remains of its site is a grassed area with a pine-covered hillock. The Tower formed part of a larger manor house, which was fortified by Roger Holden in 1422. Around the manor house lay a medieval village, mentioned in 1209, but by the late 1400s it had vanished. The name Ludworth means 'Luda's homestead'.

To the north of Shadforth, one mile away, stands the village of Sherburn Hill. Like Ludworth, it is a 19th century foundation, created to house miners after the sinking of a coal-pit. Once a bustling community, when the mine closed it became a shadow of its former self.

There is evidence from aerial photography that the first inhabitants of the parish area were Celtic Iron Age farmers. There was an Anglo-Saxon settlement of Shadforth, perhaps as far back as 800AD. The name Shadforth derives from the Old English word 'sceald', meaning shallow, and ford; thus it appears as Shaldeford in 1183. No-one knows why this early settlement disappeared, but it is likely that it was devastated during the harrying of County Durham area by the Vikings, the Scots and, just after the Conquest of 1066, by the Norman army.

The village in its present form may well have been created on the site of the lost settlement, which could explain why no trace of it has been found. It appears that the present village dates from around 1080.

The Boldon Book, a survey written for Bishop Hugh de Puiset in 1183, tells us that Shadforth, with Quarrington, Cassop, North Sherburn and South Sherburn (Sherburn House) formed the district of Quarringtonshire. Shadforth would seem to have had about 15 villeins (bond tenant farmers) and one free tenant, each holding two oxgangs of land, about 90 modern acres for some taxes, provisions and work services for the bishop. Assuming an average of one wife and two children per tenant, the population of the village would be about 64 souls.

Bishop Hatfield's survey (1345–1381) shows that about 200 years later the population remained much the same, with two free tenants, twelve bond tenants and two cottagers.

The Plough Inn, Shadforth

In the early 1600s the farmers wanted to re-organise their holdings into more easily-worked areas rather than in medieval strips of land, and in Shadforth they enclosed their new fields from 1635 onwards. These hedged enclosures gave the surrounding countryside its present shape. Life continued in much the same way for the next 200 years, but changes inevitably came.

A rising birth-rate caused Shadforth to have a population of about 180 people in 1801. It rose again to 336 by 1841. St Cuthbert's Church was consecrated 5th August, 1839 giving the village its own church, but the greatest change came when the ancient parish of Pittington (originally Pittington, Shadforth, Ludworth and Sherburn) was divided into two parishes. One of them was the whole of Shadforth township (including Ludworth) and part of Sherburn township (including Sherburn Hill) to be served as one new parish by Shadforth church.

At a stroke this created an enormous increase in the population of the parish, due to the inclusion of the new pit villages of Ludworth and Sherburn Hill where miners and their families had flooded in. It changed the character of the parish as a whole, but Shadforth itself, enclosed by steep hills and out of sight of the collieries, kept its rural aspect.

Shadforth was a thriving village in the 19th century with a National school, built 1863–4, Reading room and Library, three inns, a skinnery, shops and country tradesmen. At the turn of the century Thomas Hutchinson of the Saddle Inn was in great demand as the local pig-sticker, carrying his deadly implements and dressed in top hat. Other local characters included Mr Thubron, coffin-maker and cartwright, who had a fearsome black beard and always wore a shawl around his shoulders. Frankie Sample, another slaughterer, of Low Croft farm, well-known for hard drinking, fell off his cart on the way home one day and killed himself. One pastime, now happily ended, was sparrow shooting, which was carried out by netting the haystacks when the birds were roosting in them at night, and next morning, when the nets were loosened, the birds were blasted with shotguns.

There were wind pumps around the valley to provide water for some of the farms on higher ground, and a well at the east end of the village with steps down to the water level for the rest of the inhabitants before piped water was laid on.

Changes in agricultural methods and mechanisation between the wars had a great effect on the lives of the many villagers who depended on farming work. They drifted away to find other jobs, and the workshops of associated tradesmen closed. Farming families are now the only ones who follow the traditional country life. The rest of the working residents, many of them professional, have jobs outside Shadforth.

Two reminders of ancient days are to be found in the names of Witch Hill and Signing Bank, both near the south boundary of the parish. It seems that legend would have it that Witch Hill was the site for burnings and hangings hundreds of years ago. Signing Bank, running from Witch Hill westwards on the A181 road to Durham, was the point on the road where pilgrims, travelling from the coast to visit the shrine of St Cuthbert, first caught sight of the cathedral, and made the sign of the cross.

The village is still very attractive and has had trees planted on the green and at the outskirts. It is peaceful, quiet and pleasant, and if developers can be kept at bay it should so remain as a gem of our heritage for future generations.

Shildon

Shildon, a township situated between the rivers Wear and Tees, was first recorded during the Anglo Saxon period, when in AD821 the estate was granted to the Church. Its name was derived from the Old English Sceld or Scyld meaning shield or refuge, and dun – a hill. In 1363 the name is given as Shyldon.

The economy was strictly a rural one run by the Lord of the Manor. In 1547 the estate known as Thickley Punchardon came into the possession of the Lilburn family – known for being on the opposite side to the monarchy. Major General Robert Lilburn of Thickley Grange was one of the signatories to the death warrant of Charles I. On the other hand the Byerleys of Middridge Grange were loyal to the King. In 1717 Thickley was sold to a Londoner. We are reminded of the Lilburns and Byerleys in the street names, Byerley Road and Lilburn Close.

At the beginning of the 1800s Shildon was still merely a hamlet of little more than 100 inhabitants, in fact a map of Durham County printed in 1805 showed only a small cluster of houses at the crossroads of what is now Main Street and Byerley Road. Before the advent of the railways in 1825, men worked at collieries springing up around the area, and women and boys were employed in weaving linen and cotton which were taken to the Pease's mill in Darlington.

Large quantities of coal from West Auckland and Cockfield were brought through the village in carts and on pack-horses en route for Darlington and Stockton. Daniel Adamson's Grey Horse Inn at the crossroads did a thriving trade providing refreshment for man and beast. New means of transport were badly needed as the method used was a very expensive one. It was discovered that a horse pulling a cart on rails could haul twelve tons compared with a ton on roads, but it was not until 1814, when George Stephenson produced his first steam driven engine that an interest was shown in this means of transport. A survey of the area was made, instigated by Mr Pease, but because of much opposition it was not until 1822 that the work of constructing a line was begun. This was the beginning of the Stockton and Darlington Railway. Timothy Hackworth became Resident Engineer and the first superintendent of the first public railway which was opened on 27 September 1825. Stephenson's locomotive starting from the Mason's Arms pulled 38 wagons altogether, including a coach for directors, and 600 passengers seated on planks placed across some of the wagons for seats.

The railway works started with a complement of 20 workmen and by 1825, 50 men were employed building engines for other railways at home and abroad. The first engine in Russia was built at Shildon.

News of the workshops brought people from far and wide. Cottages were built to house these newcomers and New Shildon came into existence with its Station Street, Mechanics Street, Railway Terrace etc. By 1841 the population had increased to 2,631.

Apart from the Railway works other people were employed at Timothy Hackworth's Soho Engine Works (1832) and several at the Phoenix Brass and Iron Foundry which had recently been erected.

The Wesleyan Methodists under the leadership of Timothy Hackworth built a chapel which unfortunately adjoined the Globe Inn frequented by engine drivers. The landlord so greatly resented having a chapel next door that he made a breach through the gable and annoyed both preachers and worshippers by beating tin cans etc.

Something had to be done to improve the moral and intellectual standards of the inhabitants and as a result of a meeting led by Timothy Hackworth the idea of a Railway Institute was formed, and the school room of the chapel was used as a lecture, reading room and library. In 1842 when the Prince of Wales tunnel was opened and a new station was built, the old waiting room opposite the Masons Arms was used by the Institute.

Education was not neglected. In 1841 the Railway Company erected the British School in New Shildon. All railway employees had one penny deducted each week from their wages and each child who attended paid the usual school pence.

Due to the increase in population and the need for water for the engine boilers, a constant water supply was necessary. The problem was solved by the construction of Waskerley and Tunstall Reservoirs which were brought into use in 1871 and 1879.

St John's Church no longer met the needs of the growing community, so All Saints Church was built and opened in 1869 with an accompanying Day School opening in 1875. New industries also sprang up. The gas works were established in 1841 providing lighting for the Railway Company and Soho Works and later for street lighting. Coal was discovered in the area. Bolckow & Vaughan opened Shildon lodge Colliery in 1860, and two more deep collieries also opened – Adelaide and Dabble Duck. There were also brick works.

With the transferring of the building of locomotives to Darlington, Shildon became the chief centre for wagon building and repair – first wooden wagons, then steel. Shildon was at one time reputed to have the largest sidings in the world. In 1915 an electrified line was constructed, with overhead cables. It was built solely for moving wagons between Shildon Works and Newport, by-passing Darlington. It was 18.5 miles long, the electric engines were built at Darlington. The engine hauled 40 wagons and any child caught at the wrong side of the crossing at 8.50am each morning was invariably late for school.

What of Shildon now? The collieries have gone. Shildon Lodge is now a playing field, Adelaide a grassy slope, Dabble Duck an industrial estate. Shildon works which had its moments of glory in 1925 and again in 1975, the 150th anniversary but which closed in 1984, is now the Hackworth Industrial Park with most of the original workshops being used for other small industries. Of the four railway crossings, none now remains, but two old rail tracks have been made into pleasant walk ways. Most of the old houses originally built for railway workers and miners have been demolished and the land landscaped or built on again. Many council and private houses have been built and where the golf links were there is now a housing estate.

After the closure of Shildon Works there was an exodus of ex-employees to York, Derby and Doncaster. Some employment is found in small factories in the vicinity but some people find jobs in neighbouring towns.

Nevertheless our past lives on. We have the Timothy Hackworth museum which was opened by the Queen Mother in 1975. Very close by is the old paint shop – all that remains of Timothy Hackworth's old engine sheds – which houses a fully working replica of Hackworth's famous engine the *Sans Pareil.*

Daniel Adamson's coach house, from where he ran his own horse drawn coal service along the line built to carry coal from Shildon Lodge Colliery, is now used as a thriving community centre. The Railway Institute built in 1913 in Redworth Road is still well patronised as are the British Rail sports ground and cricket club.

The residents of Shildon are well catered for in leisure pursuits by various organisations, such as those of the Churches and Chapels, the Salvation Army, the Sunnydale Leisure Centre, the Shildon Centre, the Railway Sports and Social club, the Coach House and the Civic Hall. Shildon now has its own Comprehensive school and Leisure Centre, and with its Recreation Ground and grassed over patches and flower beds where the old dwellings used to be, it is a much more attractive place in which to live.

Shincliffe

The pleasant village of Shincliffe lies a mile and a half south east of Durham. The old village was built along a road leading down to the river Wear. The present A177 from Durham to Teesside skirts the village. Having crossed a stone bridge over the river, it climbs up a steep winding bank past the extensive newer parts now known as High Shincliffe. The character of the surrounding farmlands and woodlands has largely been maintained by the Dean and Chapter of Durham Cathedral, which has been closely associated with Shincliffe for over nine centuries. From end-to-end, Shincliffe extends for about a mile and there are now 1,197 adult residents on the electoral roll.

Shincliffe has a long history. An early record is dated 1085 when Bishop Carileph gave 'Syneclive' to the Prior and Convent of Durham. It has always been important as a river crossing. An ancient bridge decayed in 1385 and shortly after, Bishop Skirlaw (1388–1400) erected a stone bridge which stood until weakened by severe floods in 1753. The bridge in use today was built in 1824–26 and subsequently widened.

Shincliffe Village

Nearby is the site of Shincliffe Mill, whose records date from 1303; corn was ground there until 1900. During the industrial revolution coal borings were made and in 1839 Bank Top Colliery was opened. This employed 170 miners in 1851 rising to a peak of 280 five years before its closure in 1879. The railways arrived and Shincliffe then boasted two stations. The one in Shincliffe Village, opened in 1839, was also Durham City's first railway station but was closed in 1893. The Shincliffe Bank Top station survived until 1941, and the line, used for freight traffic until recently, is still there. Other activities included a sawmill and blacksmith's, one of the latter being recalled nowadays by the rose-covered house named Forge Cottage.

In 1973 a Conservation Order was issued in recognition of Shincliffe Village's natural beauty and architectural interest. Shincliffe Hall, situated in woodland near the river, was built in 1771 and is now used by

University of Durham postgraduate students. The Parish Church of St Mary the Virgin, situated in the centre of the village, was consecrated in 1851. Previously the adjoining Tithe Barn, which dated from the 17th century and can be seen from the church porch, was used as a Chapel of Ease. Shincliffe became a separate parish in 1831, formerly being part of the ancient parish of St Oswald. In 1969 community efforts raised funds for a new ring of six bells which are regularly rung by a keen group of campanologists. The organ, made by Harrison and Harrison of Durham, was installed in 1909. Next to the Rectory stands the Wesleyan Methodist Chapel, built in 1874 and still very active. There was also a United Methodist Chapel at Bank Top, opened in 1875, but this was closed in the 1930s. The first school started in 1841 at Bank Top, close to the colliery. The second opened in 1874 and, now a private residence, nestles at the foot of Shincliffe Bank. Nearly a century later, in 1968, new school buildings were completed at High Shincliffe catering well for the now expanding population.

It is known that William Stenhouse (or Sever) who was the Bishop of Durham from 1502 to 1505, was born in Shincliffe; earlier he had been Abbot of St Mary's Abbey, York (1485) and Bishop of Carlisle, (1495), and in 1496 was a Commissioner sent to Scotland to negotiate the marriage of Henry VII's daughter Margaret to James IV. Wesley preached at Shincliffe in May 1780 when stopping at Mr Parker's home. Wesley stood near the door and 'it seemed as if the whole village was ready to receive the Truth'. Willow Tree Avenue was named after a willow tree which stood near where this took place.

At present three broad strands can be recognised in the local community. There are some whose families have been in Shincliffe for several generations, some who have moved here when taking up new posts and others who have chosen to settle in Shincliffe on retirement. A wide range of occupations is represented such as agriculture and horticulture, architects and surveyors, Cathedral craftsmen and stonemasons, the medical professions, business and administration, bankers and solicitors, teachers and civil servants together with Local Authority, College and University staff and retired clergy.

There is now only one post office and general store, based at High Shincliffe, as the village post office was closed in 1981. Shincliffe Mill Boarding Kennels are on the site of the Old Mill and nearby is Shincliffe Mill Market Gardens, run by an old-established village family. On the other side of the Village the Poplar Tree Nursery forms an extensive garden centre. Most social activities take place today in the Church Hall, the Women's Institute Hut or the School Hall. A mobile library makes a fortnightly visit. The countryside walks around Shincliffe attract many ramblers who can later find respite in the three local Inns. The village is especially well worth a visit in Spring when snowdrops and daffodils line the sides of the village, linking to those planted by the Parish Council in High Shincliffe. In the 16th century, in John Leland's *Itinerary*, it was said that 'The water of Were is always of a trobelyed color, as cumminge thoroughe morishe and owrische soyles. Little or no fishe is taken but eles in the upper part of Were. For fishe can not ther well lyve in it'. Today is very different. The Durham City Angling Club says it is well populated with both game fish and coarse fish, evidence for the very opposite of the 16th century statement! It is now a clean healthy Wear flowing past an equally attractive Shincliffe.

Shotley Bridge

Though much changed over the years, the layout of the village is easily recognisable and still contributes to its charm.

Once, a century ago, a thriving hub of the community, it boasted a town hall and a spa said to have been visited by upwards of 90,000 people in a year. Charles Dickens is said to have tasted the brackish waters. Shotley Bridge owes much to the refugee sword makers from Solingen in Germany who came seeking a place where they could continue their craft.

They found the waters of the Derwent eminently suited for tempering the blades, and a supply of iron stone which later became instrumental in the setting up of the Derwent Iron Company ultimately to become the Consett Iron Company, the largest ironworks in the world, supplying steel for the building of the Sydney harbour bridge.

The Annandale family established a paper mill on the banks of the river first powered by water, later converted to steam in 1860. The paper produced had diverse uses from shirt fronts, collars and cuffs to blue sugar bags and even bibles. Many of the employees were women and a school was established for the children. Nothing now remains of the site of the mill except in local memory.

A flour mill was also owned by the Annandales, first established in the

14th century and further downstream there used to stand a gas works built in 1856.

Another local family owned the Venture coach, a coach pulled by six horses, last seen in the village in the 1960s at a fair held in the Spa grounds which now house the local cricket and tennis clubs.

The family, the Priestman's, lived at Shotley Park, and Mr Lewis Priestman was the Master of the Braes of Derwent Hunt then housed at Snowsgreen. The hunt, now at Whittonstall in Northumberland, is at least 120 years old, hunting regularly in the Derwentside area.

Jonathan Richardson, another of the local gentry was responsible for establishing the Spa which was a Hally well and a group of cottages and a bath house.

Shotley Bridge station was a mile or so up the hill from the village, not far from a local zoo from which a wolf escaped, and was hunted as far away as Carlisle before being killed on the railway line at Cumwhinton, but not before accounting for some 40 sheep on its journey.

The station was on the line from Blackhill to Newcastle which ran along the Derwent Valley, and during the Second World War a siding was built to take the wounded from Dunkirk from the train directly to what was then the Shotley Bridge Emergency Hospital which was to become one of the north's leading hospitals for open heart surgery and its burns unit which, at the time of writing, still takes some of the most severe cases for plastic surgery.

Shotley Bridge Hospital started out in life as Whinney House built in 1912 as a mental hospital. Known locally as The Colony the main blocks were later added to by temporary hutments built on the hillside. A nurses training school was added by the National Health service and it became a district general hospital with maternity, geriatric and psychiatric units added.

Shotley Park became a Dr Barnardo's Home for a number of years before becoming a nursing home. Another large house, Summerdale, a former nurses home for the local hospital staff is also now a flourishing home for the elderly.

The Piele Home, once a family owned residence was known by countless women from Tyneside and beyond as a home where mothers who were in need of a rest from childbirth were looked after, along with their children. Many young women also learned nursing and housecraft skills at the home looking after the babies and toddlers in an annex. The grounds of the home have recently become a private housing development.

The first mention of the village probably came in 1356 linked to the name of Gilbert de Brendon. The Anglicans, Methodists and Roman Catholic religions each have their own church, and there was said to have been a Quaker meeting house at Snows Green built in 1812, demolished just over a 100 years later. Quaker gravestones can still be seen at the top of Church Bank at Benfieldside.

All villages have their characters. Mad Maddison was a member of a locally respected land owning family but he was the black sheep. His notoriety is remembered in a tale that when the river was flooded he offered an old lady a lift to the other side on the back of his horse. Halfway across the wretch pushed the old lady off into the flowing torrent and the current carried her for some distance before she reached safety.

He was instrumental in killing his son in law by tying him to a horse under whose saddle he had placed some thorns. He was thrown off and killed. When his daughter re-married he tried to shoot her second husband, and he also turned to arson and larceny. Eventually he did shoot someone in a quarrel and though he escaped to Muggleswick, he was captured and taken to Durham jail.

The Grey Lady of Shotley Bridge was last seen in the village just before the Second world war but another sighting of a ghost was said to have taken place at Snows Green in the 1970s.

South Moor

Records of South Moor Colliery Company go back to 1726 but there was no village until 1840. In 1826 William Hedley became a partner with William Bell, James Morrison and George Hunter who were owners of vast coalfields in Northumberland and Durham. The same William Hedley invented the famous 'Puffing Billy' locomotive in 1813. In 1839 the company decided to open up the southern side of their coalfields.

The moor south of neighbouring Stanley was to be transformed into a working coalfield with surrounding village and so South Moor came in to existence with the sinking of the William Pit. Men from Durham, Cornwall and Norfolk came to sink the pits. From then on there was a great influx of miners and their families, which in their turn attracted tradesmen. Houses, shops, the Co-operative Society, inns and even an hotel were built as the coalfield was opened up.

South Moor Colliery Company helped to provide amenities in the village ahead of their time. There was a Miner's Welfare Hospital, Miners' Hall, Aged Miners' Homes and a Memorial Park for the fallen in the First World War with futher names added after the Second World War.

During the early years of the village the sporting and social side of life developed. Cricket, football, handball, miners' bowls, quoits, boxing and many others. Later tennis courts and a golf course were available. South Moor Brass Band was famous until 1939 having played at Belle Vue Manchester and Crystal Palace, London. A Women's Institute was formed in 1932. At one time there were three cinemas, now there are none.

Every village has its share of characters, scandals and famous visitors, South Moor is no exception. At the turn of the century three strangers came to the Smiths Arms appealing for support to the Independent Labour Party. They were later named as Keir Hardie, Cunningham Graham and George Bernard Shaw. 'Mac the Barber' (Hugh Mc Phail) came from Hamilton in Scotland in the 1890s, set up in business and became an outstanding personality for his ability to talk on any subject. His descendants still live and work in the village as hairdressers. 'Tommy's Lonnen' derived its name from a man called Tommy Daglish. He had the sole rights to gather horse manure from the lane now called Park Road.

Murder was not unknown in the history of the village. On Friday December 4th 1930, Charles Benfold, a hawker aged 39 years was found murdered in his bed. The tragedy was discovered by his wife when she returned from the cinema. Mr Benfold had been hit on the head with a heavy instrument. Mrs Jane Benfold was arrested on December 15th and committed for trial at Durham Assizes on February 16th 1931. At the trial she was found not guilty and acquitted. As far as is known the assailant was never found.

With the closure of all the mines in the area the occupations of the present population is in keeping with our modern society. Many of our workers having to travel to towns and cities for employment. Some descendants of the original miners were forced to follow in their great-grandparents' footsteps and move to all parts of the country and in some cases emigrating. In our rapidly changing world, change has come more slowly to South Moor. Many of the houses and shops still stand. Old family names still exist and the people still strive to keep the community alive.

Staindrop

Staindrop is a very pretty village on the A688 Barnard Castle to Bishop Auckland Road. Most of the houses stand back from the road with well-kept greens – it is a many-time winner of the Tidy Village Contest.

In days gone by it was the market area for the district and was mainly involved with agriculture and had a very stable population. Some of the grassed areas still have cobblestones underneath and on one area an ornamental pump still stands. It is an object of great interest to many visitors. The inscription reads IN MEMORY OF SOPHIA AND HENRY, DUKE AND DUCHESS OF CLEVELAND. A GIFT TO THE PARISH OF STAINDROP MAY 1865. As there was no piped water system in the village at that time it was a very sensible and considerate gift.

The same Duke of Cleveland – occupier of Raby Castle in the year 1860 used a piece of ground called Cathric's Garth, and built upon it twelve almshouses to be occupied by poor persons above the age of 60. Each person, or one of a couple was paid £5 per quarter – £20 pa – being considered sufficient to maintain a person living rent and rates free. When the first person moved into the houses in 1861, Lady Augusta, sister of the duchess gave an armchair to each house. These almshouses have recently been modernised and are all occupied by people over 60 who now pay a modest amount towards the maintainance of the property. They are still looked after by 'The Duke of Cleveland Charity Trust'.

Standing as they do behind the houses of the main street, and one looking over open fields, it is a quiet tranquil area of a now busy village.

Stanhope

Stanhope is known as the capital of Upper Weardale and is situated at a crossroad linking Durham to the east, Alston to the west, Hexham to the north and Barnard Castle to the south.

In the market place of this stone built attractive village one can picture its history from prehistoric times. In front of the 12th century Norman church, there is a fossilized tree dating from the carboniferous age which was found on the nearby moors. In the 19th century in caves near Stanhope Burn, Bronze Age relics were found. These are now to be found in the British Museum. Whilst in Stanhope one can find evidence that the Romans visited Weardale; possibly to mine for the lead and silver in the surrounding hillsides.

In later years lead mining and quarrying were to be the main sources of income and employment, engulfing some of the agricultural land that was used for farming.

Behind the church is the Stone House, a former rectory and one of the oldest houses in Stanhope. In front of the church is the Market Cross where John Wesley preached to large crowds. To the west is Stanhope Castle, built in 1798 on the ruins of a former fortified building. Next to the church were the castle gardens, which have now been converted to the Durham Dales Centre, which hosts several craft and workshops, an information centre and cafe.

Immediately to the east of the Market Cross is the Bonny Moor Hen. A pub which hosted the bloody Battle of Stanhope, between the Bishop of Durham's men and the local poachers (miners) who caught grouse to supplement their diet.

Opposite is the Pack Horse Inn from which the Rob Roy stage coach regularly ran. Today we are well served with a bus service. We have an industrial railway line, but during the summer months the Heritage line runs a passenger train from Saltburn to Stanhope along a scenic riverside route.

Just past the Bonny Moor Hen there is a good variety of shops, opposite an ancient walk lined with old lime trees. Behind the old stone walls is the Old Rectory, part of which is the church hall – an invaluable meeting place for the many village organisations. Walking back along Limetree Walk and turning to the river, one encounters The Butts, the old area once reserved for practising archery. Continuing along a beautiful, treelined, riverside walk leads to a park and an open air swimming pool. Here there are stepping stones to cross the ford to Unthank Hall and Unthank Farm. The field behind is used on the second weekend in September for a large Agricultural show which has been held for over 150 years and is the highlight of the village year.

Retracing over the stepping stones past local hospitals and then turning west, one comes to an old medieval manor house, once home to the Featherstonhaugh family but now an hotel and restaurant.

Stanhope is a popular place to visit for the day, or to use as a base for touring the Northern Pennines, that last wilderness of Britain, in the heart of the Land of the Prince Bishops.

Startforth

Startforth is situated on the south side of the river Tees, opposite Barnard Castle, at a place where the Roman road from Binchester to Bowes crossed the river, hence the name Steetford or Stratford corrupted in later times to Startforth. Until the county boundary changes in 1974 the river divided Durham from the North Riding of Yorkshire.

Below where the Romans crossed the river a two arched bridge was built in 1569 and is still in use today carrying the A67 road and joining the village to Barnard Castle. In days gone by there was a chapel in the centre of the bridge and in it the notorious Cuthbert Hilton celebrated illicit marriages. He did this by holding out a broomstick and asking the couple to jump over it holding hands while he repeated the rhyme:

> 'My blessings on your pates, and your groats in my purse
> You are never the better and I am never the worse'.

His argument was that whilst the pair were in mid air over the boundary they were not under the jurisdiction of either Durham or York.

There are two footbridges over the river. The one upstream of the old stone bridge was built in 1893 by the Stockton and Middlesbrough Water Company and carries the water mains from the reservoirs and treatment plant higher up the valley to the communities near the river mouth. The other footbridge was built in 1882 and replaced an earlier structure which had been washed away in a great flood on 9th March the previous year.

There is no centre, such as a green, as there is to many of the dales villages. It is divided into three distinct parts: High Startforth, Low Startforth and Bridge End. The parish also includes the small hamlet of Egglestone Abbey half a mile down the river.

In the 18th and early 19th centuries there were two or three of the 'Yorkshire Schools' made famous by Charles Dickens in *Nicholas Nickleby* to be found in the village, and until recently it was possible to see the names and dates of some of the unfortunate pupils scratched on the window panes and lead roof flashings of a house in High Startforth which had been used for this purpose.

The present village school caters for children up to 11 years old in the best of modern buildings. It was created by extending the original structure which dated from 1877 and was built as a memorial to Ellen Frances Morritt of Rokeby. The initials and the date can be seen above the doorways leading into the original building. Over the years there have been many well respected and long serving members of staff at the school. Robert Bailey was headmaster from 1885 to 1926, 41 years, Elizabeth Watson taught there for 40 years and Mary Plews was a scholar, pupil teacher and member of staff from 1885 until she died still in service in 1942, a total of 57 years.

The church, dedicated to the Holy Trinity, was built in 1863 replacing a much earlier one on the same site which was mentioned in The Domesday Book (1086). Nothing remains of the original other than the font, a monumental effigy thought to represent Helen de Hastings, and a few carved stones. The font is thought to date from about 1484 as it bears the letters R and K which may refer to King Richard III who only reigned from 1483–85. The font of the parish church in Barnard Castle is almost identical. Both are carved from 'Tees Marble' which was quarried from the river gorge near Egglestone Abbey.

The ruins of Egglestone Abbey are in a beautiful setting high above the river and were the subject of a painting by Turner. Near the Abbey is a 75 ft high single arched bridge over the Tees in a most spectacular setting. It was built in 1773 by John Morritt of Rokeby Hall as a Toll Bridge and stayed as such until recently. The foundations of the keepers cottage can be seen with the bedroom on one side of the road and the living quarters on the other.

The Feilding family purchased lands and property in and around Startforth during the reign of Elizabeth I (1558–1603) and nearly 400 years later their descendants still live in High Startforth Hall. In the churchyard there are a number of memorials to past family members.

Until the 1920s there was a factory in the village owned by Ullathorne and Co who specialised in the manufacture of linen thread for the shoe and sailmaking industries. At its busiest up to 200 people worked there, the buildings have now been demolished and the site landscaped to form a popular picnic area overlooking the old bridge and the river. In earlier times there were two water powered corn mills in the village and a mill near Egglestone Abbey that produced paper.

Startforth for many years had associations with the army, starting in the early 1800s when a rifle range was constructed in the Deepdale Beck valley which borders the village. In its early years it was used by the Teesdale Volunteers raised to help protect the country against Napoleon.

Ullathorne & Co Linen Thread Mill, Startforth

Later it was used by the Durham Militia who had barracks in Barnard Castle and then by the Durham Light Infantry. After the First World War it became overgrown but was quickly brought back into use in 1939.

The fields near the ranges were originally used as a tented camping area but in 1939 a more permanent brick built complex was built and was home to many regiments for many years during and after the war. Many ex-servicemen up and down the country have memories both good and bad of Deerbolt Camp.

For the last ten years Deerbolt has been an Institute for Young Offenders and will no doubt be remembered by the inmates.

Tanfield

The original church in this village and a pub said to have entertained Cromwell, were built more than 700 years ago. The recently restored Tranfield Railway has the distinction of being the oldest surviving railway in the world, travelling to the oldest railbridge in the world at Causey Arch.

The railway was built by a consortium of local mine owners known as the Grand Allies and originally carried horse drawn waggons. They had wooden wheels which often were set alight by sparks on the steep gradients down to the river Tyne from Tanfield Moor and their precious hard won cargo of coal only added fuel to the fire!

The bridge built in 1727 has survived despite the fact that the builder Ralph Wood was said to have committed suicide from it when he realised he had omitted the keystone.

Tantobie

In the first edition of the 'History of Durham' published by Francis Whellan in 1856, Tantoby (note the spelling) is described as a hamlet in the Beamish Township, nine miles south-west of Newcastle. It lies north-west of Tanfield Lea and except for a small number of houses to the west is comparatively recent. There is no mention in any of the ancient vestry records and in the church records it is spelled 'Tantove'. Up to the 16th century it was known as Wester Leigh. 'Leigh' is the former spelling of Tanfield Lea. It seems to have formed an important centre of population as it had a Co-operative Society prior to 1870 and a post office prior to 1880. Annfield Plain Co-operative society came into being in 1870 and prior to that the members had enlisted the help of the Tantobie Co-operative Society's members for their guidance in the formation of the new society.

Old maps show dwellings on the south side of the road which passes through the village and joins the Tanfield to Pickering Nook Road. Subsequent development was in the form of long streets on the north side of the road. Employment in mining was at the Tanfield Moor colliery situated to the west of Tantobie. An interesting fact which has been recorded is that in Tantobie lived Mrs Meggie Turner, a woman employed by the colliery company to awaken miners in the early hours to get them off to work. The Hare Law to Tanfield Moor Colliery wagon way was opened in 1843. One of Thomas Newcomen's original pumping engines, first patented in 1705, was sited here for more than 120 years and pumped water 200 feet up the workings of Tanfield Moor colliery.

In 1928 new offices for the Tanfield Urban District Council were built at the foot of the long streets mentioned above. The offices faced on to the Tanfield Lea to Pickering Nook Road. The building cost £3,500.

The only other reference in Whellan is that 'here is a Wesleyan Chapel and a goods station on the North Eastern Railway.'

In Whellan's second edition of the *History of Durham* there is a description of the Wesleyan Chapel as a handsome stone building, erected in 1893, to seat 330, at a cost of over £1,000. It is a neat building of Early English design with a Sunday-school below and is well-fitted in pitch pine.

Following this there is a description of the Primitive Methodist Chapel erected in 1876, being of brick construction, seating 370 and costing £955 to erect.

There are two inns in the village, named the Commercial and the Oak Tree. The road through the village joins the Tanfield Lea to Pickering Nook road and continues towards Tanfield Village. As the road proceeds towards the village it passes on its right the small conurbation of houses named 'Sleepy Valley'. Proceeding onwards there is a building formerly used as an isolation hospital in the late 1920s and early 1930s. In the main it was used for the treatment of children suffering from scarlet fever or diphtheria. Parents and visitors to the children were only allowed to see the children through the closed windows of the hospital ward. The hospital was later used as a garment factory which was subsequently modernised in 1967.

The Tantobie Women's Institute formerly held its meetings in a disused colliery engine house which had been adapted for the purpose. The Institute now meets in a communal building provided by the local authority. Notable personalities were a Mr Lynch and Mr Jack Weightman. The former became a member of the Metropolitan Police in 1886 and retired in 1914. He became involved in many of the more serious crimes such as 'Jack the Ripper' and Dr Crippen.

The other personality was Mr Jack Weightman, a member of the British Transport Police for 41 years. He was considered to be a very strong man, able to lift very heavy weights and is alleged to have been able to knock a six inch nail through a three inch plank of wood.

Toft Hill

Toft Hill is on the A68–it stands 700 feet above sea level, commanding panoramic views of Weardale to the north, where Durham Cathedral and Penshaw monument can be seen on a clear day. To the south, we can see Teesdale and the distant hills of Swaledale.

In the post-war years Durham County council gave it the infamous title of 'Category D', which meant some of the older condemned dwellings were demolished, but not replaced. Happily, in the last decade, infill building has been allowed, mainly on old sites and a new estate created at Southfield Park. Most of the houses were miners' cottages which have been tastefully modernised.

Mining was the main occupation of the villagers, who travelled to the surrounding mines to work. The name of Mr Maines was associated and lived at Toft Hill Hall. Since these mines ceased operation, periods of open cast mining to the north and south of the village took place, in the course of which, 'Allendene Farm', brought down the desired stone and coal in a tunnel below, and the wrath of farmer and Mrs Dent above! The noise and force of the explosion shook the foundations of the house.

The Luftwaffe did not neglect Toft Hill, for on 15th August 1940, a bombing raid killed Willie Harrison (an evacuee) on the steps of the Social Centre, he came from Hebburn (for safety). The same day bombs caused chaos in Etherley Churchyard disturbing the grave of Robert Mothershaw who in 1916 had died in the Red House Military Hospital of wounds inflicted by the enemy in the First World War.

Mr J. S. Tallentire was the first to provide a transport service from Bishop Auckland to Hamsterley. The Belsize bus had acetylene headlamps, solid tyres, could be used with an open top in summer and being a joiner he made a roof for winter. Other operators were 'Griffiths', 'Prospect', 'Osborne Limited', and now only 'OK' operate. In 1946 the return fare was 6 pence, now £1.44 from Toft Hill.

Toft Hill School was opened in 1915 then made a junior and later also an infants school.

In 1934 unemployed miners began an ambitious project which ended successfully in the conversion of a disused quarry into a playing field, tennis courts, bowling green and children's recreation ground. Today only a football pitch remains. The men used picks and shovels to remove an estimated 20,000 tons of stone for only 9 pence a day; this stone was used in building the Social Centre in 1936. It was completed and opened by Sir Henry Pelam and the children's playground was opened by the Duke of Kent. In 1975 a Community Association was formed to modernise the building with various ways of raising money – selling bricks £1, coffee mornings, waste paper collection, donations and some financial grants from County and Local Councils. This was completed and reopened on 22 May 1976. It is well used by whist drives, old time dance, bingo, over 60s club, wedding receptions, Womens Institute, etc.

More than twenty kinds of tradesmen sought a living from an inadequate money supply. Gypsies camped on Toft Hill High Quarry, so tinkers, knife grinders, scrap merchants and organ grinders managed a living. We still have three general stores, a post office, a filling station and two garages.

Today, many inhabitants are unknown to each other, spend little time in the village, having to travel to work in shops, factories, hospitals and schools.

We have a very active Carnival Committee who organise a Carnival and Autumn Fair in order to give our senior citizens a Christmas dinner, gifts and money. The Age Concern Luncheon Club manned by faithful teams has been functioning since 1973.

Our most urgent need is a By-Pass promised imminently.

Tow Law

Straddling the A68 road from Scotch Corner to Edinburgh, high in the hills lies the hardly graceful village of Tow Law – the place locals joke about as being 'the place that God forgot'. Tow Law might not be a pretty place but its local people are warm, it is bustling, and it still boasts a weekly mart where stock is sold, often as briskly as the wind which blows unstoppably across the Pennines.

The area is used to harsh winter weather and in recent times a tragedy occurred when an elderly man and his sister set off to walk home along a country road, just as it started to snow heavily. They perished in deep drifts.

Victorian astronomer Thomas Espin was vicar here from 1888 to 1934. He was the author and editor of a number of works about astronomy who built an observatory in his garden.

Trimdon Station

Trimdon Station is the offspring of the Trimdon Village which was the original Trimdon. Trimdon Grange is also another branch of the parent village. The three Trimdons can be very confusing to strangers. The word Trimdon is commonly thought to have derived from the time when King Canute in 1020 got off his horse at this spot, had his head shaved and travelled barefooted to the shrine of St Cuthbert at Durham.

Another version is that the word Trem came from a personal name of a Warwickshire Hundred. In the Boldon Book it was known as 'Treme-duna'. Trimdon Colliery or New Trimdon was included in Deaf Hill-Cum-Langdale parish and lies 591 feet above sea level to the west of Trimdon.

The rainfall is moderate and the air bracing and clear. An old custom was to take children suffering from whooping cough to stand on the Hilly Howley where it was supposed seven airs met.

The Colliery Rows houses with one large downstairs kitchen and one garret bedroom, reached by ladder-like stairs, were in close streets with the doors opening straight onto the road. Parents slept downstairs, often in a fourposter bed facing the door. When there was a death in the family the corpse was laid on the trestles at the foot of the bed. In one such house in Lord Street the sympathisers were all crowded in the kitchen one dusky evening when a young girl looking for a resting place, backed onto the bier and accidently caused the bier and the corpse to stand up. Needless to say the crowded kitchen was very soon empty.

The men worked at the pit. Deaf Hill Colliery was sunk by the Trimdon Coal company in 1870. My dad started work there as a 14 years old boy and worked there until he retired at 65 in 1965. The men travelled home from work each day black and got bathed at home until the Pit Head Bath opened. However, dad would not use them, saying 'I've travelled black all these years and I'm not getting bathed in front of the other men'. His bait was always the same – a tin bottle of water and jam and bread sandwiches carried in a tin box (to protect from the mice).

Deaf Hill Colliery closed in February 1967 and the Pit heap was removed and shafts filled in. Now it is green fields and no one would know that a colliery had been there.

Mr Fred Hope was the ambulance attendant at Deaf Hill Colliery for many years, and was awarded the BEM in 1955. He was well known to all the villagers, who took their children to be treated at his home and was looked on as a doctor.

At Trimdon Colliery there was Coffee Pot Street with a huge coffee pot hanging as a sign. Tank Street was named after a big tank kept there for drawing water.

Byers Field between Trimdon Colliery and Trimdon Grange was once the place of cow byers. The Foundry, as it is still called today, was so named because a forge was once there before its transfer to Spennymoor.

For years the local chemist was T. L. Scott, Esquire, and people from far and near travelled for his advice and treated him as their doctor. He was also the local tooth extractor.

Leather Watson, a Boot and Shoe Man, was another highly esteemed man for he made and sold a very good rubbing bottle.

John Edwards, a Trimdon Grange man, and fruiterer by trade was the first to introduce bananas into Trimdon at the turn of the century.

Trimdon Village & Trimdon Grange

Trimdon Village is at the top of the 'Watch Bank' on the B1278 road about three miles north of Sedgefield. It is a medieval village with a Norman church on a mound in the village centre. The church, St Mary Magdalene, has a splendid 'keyhole arch' and what may be a 'Leper Window'. More recently, during repair work, archaeologists looking for a tunnel, found a burial chamber with five coffins beneath the chancel floor. The coffins belonged to the Beckwith family, and after the chamber was photographed for records, it was resealed and a new floor laid. South-east of the church in the burial ground is the monument to the 83 men and boys killed in the Trimdon Grange mining explosion of 1882.

Fiction writer Mary Stewart spent some of her childhood in Trimdon Village when her father was the vicar.

Trimdon Grange takes its name from nearby Trimdon Village and the 'Grange' the local mine owner's home.

Once known locally as 'Fire House' it has a station and level-crossing. The pit was sunk about 1840 and following the explosion at 2.30 pm on February 16th, 1882, George Robson, a 13 year old survivor of the disaster, wrote a poem of which the following is an extract:

> 'Now whether my companions have gone to heaven is not for me to say,
> Although they cried for mercy before they passed away.
> Yet the thief upon the cross was saved at the eleventh hour,
> And I hope to meet my companions upon your golden shore'.

George Robson died in 1935, the last survivor of the disaster. He was a local Methodist preacher, Alderman and friend of Peter Lee, who was brought up at 5 Duff Heap Row, and of Ramsay Macdonald.

Tursdale

Tursdale is situated between Coxhoe and Ferryhill and was the site of a thriving colliery. A street of houses and a school was built to accommodate the miners' families but when the mine closed (as well as the school) a large new training centre was built by the NCB and now serves the few remaining collieries in the county as an engineering workshop. Several farms surround the village and the large house now named 'The Grange' was originally 'Hoggersgate House' as this was built at the edge of the wood wherein roamed the remaining wild hogs of the district.

On the beck at Tursdale there was a mill (now a restaurant) and between there and Croxdale there were at one time seven working mills all worked from the same beck. Latterly a map of this beck and a legal document (in Latin) from the 15th century came to light in the archives of Durham Cathedral. This document disputed the amount of water taken by one mill to the detriment of another at Hett Mill.

We are told there were flour, paper and worsted mills on this short stretch of water, less than two miles in length, including Tursdale Mill, Hett Mill and Croxdale Mill.

On the hill above Hett Mill stands Tursdale House. Once the Manor House of the district it dates back to the 12th century and belonged in the latter centuries to the Naworths (relatives of the Castle Howard family) and to one Esquire Wilkinson of Durham. In the 18th century the estate was allowed to fall into disrepair and the manor house was reduced to the farm house as it is today. On the 15th century map it is shown as a castellated building and the farm buildings now gone suggested a prosperous dwelling. As Tursdale House is on the old coach road from Ferryhill to Shincliffe its own smithy stood until the 1950s. At that time you could count 5 pit heaps – but now they are all gone, the land reclaimed and well landscaped; certainly an improvement brought about by Durham County Council to enhance our beautiful county.

Ushaw

The name of Ushaw College is known throughout the Roman Catholic world as a seminary. Now part of Durham University, this lofty hill top college is the successor of the college founded at Douai in Northern France and destroyed during the French Revolution.

North West Durham has played host to many refugees including the monks of Douai who fled to Crook Hall near Consett, and who went on to found their new college at Ushaw.

Waldridge Fell

The name is thought to mean 'cultivation riggs by the wall' which probably describes a small village built up to the wall which surrounded the Bishop of Durham's hunting park – ie the fells. The Bishop's stables were built in the village and he used the now fell land as a racecourse. These rights were either handed down or bought by the Earl of Durham.

The early cottages were built in the 1830s and followed the course of the Cong Burn, giving the impression that it was probably used as the water supply. Most of these cottages have been demolished and replaced by terraced housing built in the late 19th century. There were two chapels, a church and an inn called The Swan, now known as The Tavern. The Workmen's Club, which every village had, was built against the wishes of the Colliery Manager, so was sited down in the valley, which had the added advantage of helping the inebriated to sober up while climbing back up the bank to return home.

Two schools were built but together with many of the other buildings have been demolished. The Methodist Chapel, a beautiful stone building, built with sandstone from the local quarry, has been modernised and is now a guest house enjoyed by visitors. The land of Waldridge has been undermined in many places for coal, thus providing the local people with employment in the mines, the quarries and the brick works. Some of the workings were closed down during the General Strike in 1926.

The Colliery Manager domineered the village people and because he once missed the train from Chester-le-Street to Newcastle-on-Tyne he then decided that all clocks would be put forward by one hour, thus making the six o'clock buzzer sound at five o'clock, and he never missed his train again.

Crisscrossing the village was a series of railways or wagonways used to carry the coal to its destination. One such wagonway runs from nearby Sacriston and on to Pelton Fell. This was built upon a Roman aqueduct, taking water from the higher springs to the Roman fort at Chester-le-Street.

Skirting the village on two sides are the South Burn and the Cong Burn which join in the river Wear at Chester-le-Street. The latter Long Burn runs through an ancient glacial valley where special plants and a wide variety of animals are to be found and rock formation can be seen and studied.

The last of the mine shafts was blown up in 1963 by the Television Corporation whilst making the film *Germinal* from the novel by the French author, Emile Zola. Many of the villagers took part in this as extras, thus making themselves some pin money.

There is very little evidence of the mining remaining. The spoil heaps have been reclaimed and planted with vegetation in tune with the surroundings.

The fell land surrounding the village on three sides now covers an area of 300 acres and is the last surviving lowland heath in County Durham.

Its history can be traced back when, like most of Durham, it was covered in woodland which was burned off by early Iron Age settlers and since has been burned at least twice more. Due to the action of wind and rain it turned into an acid soil which grows acid loving plants such as heather, gorse, bracken, bilberry, and crowberry. At various times over the centuries this land has been used for grazing of cattle, sheep and goats. About fifty years ago, many of the villagers had goats, pigs, hens and rabbits to eke out their frugal life-style. The village was then known affectionately by their neighbours as 'nanny-goat land'.

Over the years Waldridge has changed from a mining to a residential village with no industry and little to remind one of its past. The population is mixed – teachers, plumbers, builders, doctor etc.

At the end of the day, Waldridge, though it may be old-fashioned and not quite as posh as other places, is a lovely healthy place to live and we love it.

Waterhouses

Waterhouses, now a quiet village nestling in the Deerness Valley, takes its name from a medieval dwelling built in the reign of Elizabeth I by a family called Claxton, who were retainers of Charles Neville, Earl of Westmorland and Lord of Brancepeth.

The Claxtons were staunch Catholics and they paid a heavy price for their faith both in church fines and imprisonment for non-attendance at an Anglican Church. It was necessary to pursue their religion secretly and one priest in particular officiated in the Deerness Valley. John Boste, a former lecturer in logic at Queen's College, Oxford, and admitted to the priesthood in France, is known to have visited a number of houses on the Brancepeth Estate and he worked actively to persuade the northern Catholics to support Mary, Queen of Scots, instead of Queen Elizabeth.

In September, 1593, John Boste was arrested having said Mass at the Waterhouse. During the raid, the searchers, frustrated in their aim, broke open some walling of the house and found the priest in a hiding place. William Claxton was absent – in prison at the time – but Lady Margaret Neville and Mrs Grace Claxton were both arrested and, under the laws against harbouring priests, charged with treason. Both were found guilty. Lady Margaret was eventually pardoned after she gained the support of the Bishop of Durham who believed he had converted her from her former ways. Once free, she reverted to Catholicism.

Grace Claxton was sentenced to death by hanging but she was reprieved on the grounds that she was pregnant. This was confirmed by an examination carried out by eight women and she was pardoned on 30th June 1594. She returned to the Waterhouse where she farmed in order to support her husband whose loyalty to his faith was undiminished with a consequent increase in unpaid fines and further terms of imprisonment.

John Boste was imprisoned for a time in the Tower of London and later returned to Durham where he was found guilty of treason, hung, drawn and quartered at Dryburn. He was beatified in 1929, created a saint by the Pope in 1970 and is commemorated in a painting, which hangs in Ushaw College. The triptych, painted in 1937 by Geoffrey Webb, shows, on the one side, the martyrs of the Northern Dioceses and, on the other, the Douai Martyrs, including John Boste, grouped around the central figure of St Thomas More.

The site of the Waterhouse itself cannot be precisely identified. Today there are two farms of Waterhouse, High and Low, on the north bank of the Deerness. A map of 1701 shows a building between these two but on the south bank of the river and this may be The Waterhouse. Unfortunately, this structure no longer survives.

Research of John Boste's life was undertaken by Norman Emery and published in a paper entitled *St John Boste and The Waterhouse* (1982).

Wearhead

It is not difficult to trace the origin of the name of Wearhead, a few yards upstream from the bridge, right in the middle of the village, the Killhope and Burnhope Burns converge, forming the river Wear which flows down Weardale, through Durham city, to reach the sea at Sunderland.

In 1300 it is recorded in the Palatinate records that there was a farm settlement at Wearhead but an actual village did not exist until the late 18th century when most of the cottages were built, constructed from the locally quarried, hand-hewn sandstone. In the early 19th century, as the lead mining industry grew, more housing was required to accommodate an increasing population.

The present day village has not grown significantly since the end of the 19th century apart from the addition of a small council house estate and one or two bungalows. Most of the houses line the A689 which is the main road through Weardale, to Alston and Cumbria, via Killhope, where it is the highest main road in England.

Wearhead nestles alongside the river. The layout of the village was never planned – it just happened – the houses lying higgledy-piggledy as if dropped from above by a giant hand. Steep sided slopes cradle it in a valley gouged out in the Ice Age. The breathtaking beauty of the surrounding fells, the abundance of wild flowers, the view from the bridge, spring born lambs in fields within touching distance, the fragrance on a summer's morning of new-mown hay, all these continue to be part of everyday life in this small, virtually unspoilt corner of Durham.

To the west of the village there is a south-east facing wooded hillside. In spring it is covered in a carpet of wild primroses, where, if you are lucky enough, in the quiet of an early morning you may glimpse a grazing roe deer amongst the trees.

At 1,100 ft above sea level Wearhead is very much a prey to the elements, particularly in winter. It has seen many storms with blocked roads and power cuts. Locals still tell tales of the 'big storms' of '47, '63 and '79. In 1947 all the coal was carried from the station on sledges; farmers tell of walking the animals along the wall tops because the snow was too deep in the fields to travel through; local men unable to go to their normal work, hand cut the drifts blocking all the roads, forming walls of snow 15 feet high. In 1963 fodder had to be dropped by aeroplane to starving sheep on the fells. In 1979 life was made a little easier by the use of the newly-invented snow blowers which were pioneered in Weardale. Accustomed to severe weather conditions, farmers on the surrounding hills tend their flocks in frequently sub-arctic conditions. On the other hand there are numerous gloriously bright frosty days when Wearhead is above the freezing fog which covers the rest of the county.

Wearhead has always been a close-knit community. Until quite recently anyone coming from more than ten miles away was an 'incomer'. The fact that it is virtually surrounded by hills tended, in days gone by, to exaggerate the feeling of being isolated – thus fostering a strongly independent character in the residents. The surrounding 'dales' of Allendale and Teesdale were referred to as 'ower the top'. Many people from other parts of the country have now bought houses and settled in the village, whereas younger people, unable to find work or affordable housing, are tending to move away.

Nevertheless the community feeling still continues and Wearhead has a thriving social life, with activities connected with both church and chapel, a football team, Women's Institute, carpet bowls club, Day Club, Horticultural Society and a Village Hall which is used most nights of the week.

This is a small community trying to preserve its character and way of life in rapidly changing times, with the 'supermarket' only half an hour's drive away, Europe's largest indoor shopping centre at Gateshead less than an hour away. The social structure has so far remained intact, the sheer beauty of the area, the easy pace of life, the friendliness of the people and the indomitable Weardale character will hopefully preserve Wearhead for many years to come.

West Cornforth

The village of West Cornforth was at first called New Thrislington until 1857 when it took the present one. The first colliery which had been sunk in 1835 closed in 1851. In 1859 an Iron Works had opened and in 1867 Thrislington Colliery was sunk. This caused a population explosion. In 1851 the population was 1040 and by 1871 it was 3416 which necessitated the building of numerous streets of houses. Then followed shops, public houses, and then chapels and a Salvation Army and a Roman Catholic church. The colliery closed in 1966 which dealt a death blow to the village. Many of the shops are now closed except for the CWS only a shadow of its former self. The village around 1870 looked set to become a small town with the founding of the Iron Works as Spennymoor had done. During that time the blast furnaces there had the biggest blast furnace in the world.

Besides the above the village had an Iron Foundry and Coke Works. All traces of these and the colliery were removed in 1971 when all the area was landscaped.

Westgate in Weardale

Westgate village consists of two main parts. High Westgate, which is the older, and Westgate Village. At High Westgate a Small Castle or Hunting Lodge was built by the Prince Bishops of Durham during their grand visits into Weardale – forerunners of the present day trippers perhaps, who come into the Dale still searching for wildlife – though, hopefully not for the pot!

Their search will usually be rewarded up Slit Wood – an area of pleasant walks, waterfalls, and old lead mining remains.

The main part of the village is concentrated along the A689 which runs through Westgate, with a clutch of quaint sounding names – Britton and Shallowford, Waterside and Windyside, Weeds and Haswicks.

We are fortunate to have a well stocked Co-op/post office as well as a butchers, filling station and public house.

We also have the oldest, perhaps the only, Subscription Library to be still in use. It was formed over 200 years ago by the lead miners; poor, but determined to use some of their hard-won pay to create a library. The rules, governing the type of literature to be available – 'of an essentially religious and moral nature' – still survive today. The subscription is now sixty pence per year!

The youth of Westgate are lucky to have a play area on the site of the old Railway Station. The waiting room is now a club house, with hard court outside and grass where the track once ran beside the river.

The Village Hall provides a venue for the local indoor bowls team and pensioners club, while a Methodist chapel and Anglican church afford ample opportunity for worship. All this in a village of barely 300 souls!

This number increases, of course, during summer time and weekends when a number of visitors take up temporary residence in various caravans, holiday cottages and bed and breakfast accommodation. Today there is a marked increase in the latter as tourists from further afield are discovering more and more an area which has been until recently largely unknown.

Westgate's annual events include an Easter Fayre, organised by the youth of the village, as is the RISK, an exciting run and obstacle race, followed by a tennis tournament and football knockout held in July. This is closely followed by a village Fun Day – a Carnival event for children.

In August the Village Hall plays host to an auction – bargains for everyone! Westgate Leek Club holds its show in September, followed in October by the Methodist chapel's bazaar.

The youth of the village come to the fore again in November with a communal bonfire, and by now they are busy rehearsing for the Christmas Pantomime.

Throughout the year St Andrew's church holds a series of coffee mornings, the Pensioners club are going off on outings, and the WI are enjoying their monthly meetings!

Flowering cherry trees screen the caravan site along the roadside while the fields beyond the dry stone walls are full of spring lambs, grazing cattle, or wild flowers awaiting hay time.

Westgate is a place where some come to walk, some to visit, some to fish and some to play but best of all some come to stay.

Whorlton

Whorlton is situated on the north bank of the Tees four miles downstream from Barnard Castle. The original name was Querington, derived from the quarries which for centuries provided the local building stone. The Parish of Whorlton (population 205) consists of houses built round a triangular green, various out-lying farms and Sledwich, an Elizabethan house of some distinction. The village is surrounded by tall trees, the steep banks to the river being heavily wooded.

Whorlton has a long history, being a local crossing point of the Tees for many centuries. Originally there was a ford to Wycliffe and beyond. But this was dangerous, and a ferry-boat operating from 1691 proved equally so. A public house (The 'Boot and Shoe') stood at the water's edge, and there were many accidental drownings on dark nights!

Relief came, however, with the erection of the present suspension bridge, opened amid great rejoicing in 1831. Built by John Green of Newcastle, it is the oldest suspension bridge in the country supported unaided by its original chains, and is still in constant use, in spite of a tendency to sway under the movement of tramping feet along its wooden roadway and pavements! Recently a three ton limit for vehicles has been imposed to preserve this remarkable structure. The ford was blown up soon after the opening, but the ferry remained until the 1850s. The Bridge was controlled by tolls until after the First World War; it and the toll house are now listed buildings.

In this same year, 1831, the village population peaked at 311. Improved communications resulted in much activity. A school, built in 1848, was enlarged in 1870 to accommodate 100 children, many coming from across the river. Whorlton Sports Day in 1867 records 19 events, with 157 entrants, competing for valuable cash and other prizes. In 1887 a drinking fountain was erected near the school to commemorate Queen Victoria's Golden Jubilee.

In 1894 the population of 245 included, among others: two publicans, a butcher, tailor, joiner, mason, farm bailiff, blacksmith and overseer, bricklayer, shopkeeper, schoolmaster, vicar and eight farmers. A busy community!

In the 19th century there were two places of worship. The Parish Church was built in 1853 (at a cost of £600!) on the site of the old flat-roofed chapel-of-ease at the south end of the green. An Independent

Whorlton Village Hall and Drinking Fountain

Chapel built nearby in 1840 is now the Parish Hall, owned by the Church and leased to the Whorlton Village Community Association. The church building, having an octagonal spirelet with a single bell, can accommodate 150 people and is a good example of Victorian architecture with very fine stained glass. It is surrounded by the churchyard and bordered by tall wellingtonias to the south.

Baptisms long ago could be hazardous. In 1644 the font broke, diverting infant ceremonies to Barnard Castle. But in 1645 the plague there forced everyone back to Whorlton! The broken font is today a listed monument.

In the 1850s the vicar of Whorlton, the Rev A. W. Headlam, built

Whorlton Hall (30 rooms, including 17 bedrooms) both as an educational coaching establishment for students wishing to enter University and for his own occupation. The hall remained in the Headlam family until 1977.

It is now a nursing home for mentally handicapped adults. There are ghosts at Whorlton Hall, including a 'laundry ghost' who on one or two occasions did some knitting at night!

Whorlton's present day population is mainly retired, commuting or farming. There are two nursing homes, one already mentioned and one for elderly people; the Bridge Inn, a bed and breakfast establishment, and a garage a mile from the village. Whorlton is fortunate in having someone who can turn his hand to most jobs – gardening, decorating, minor repairs. The church is lively and provides good social activities. The parish hall is used by the PCC, the Parish Council, and particularly the WI as well as for private parties. There is a thrice-yearly newsletter, and social activities including Guy Fawkes bonfire and fireworks and a Village Day with sports, barbecue and dancing are organized by the Village Association. Across the bridge is Whorlton Lido, where people come to enjoy the beautiful stretch of river, the miniature railway and children's playground. Over the years the village has won frequent awards in the County Council 'Tidy Village Competition'.

The beautiful setting of Whorlton encourages many who live beyond its bounds to join in village activities, just as they have done over the centuries, to the mutual benefit of all.

Witton Gilbert

In early times circa AD547 the village was known as 'Witun' so that it is obviously of Saxon origin. The Saxon word 'tun' means a fortified place and 'wit' was the shortened form of white, hence White Town became Witun. The spelling varied until finally it was Witton.

The village of Witton Gilbert, pronounced Jilbert, is situated 3½ miles north west of Durham City. It nestles in the Browney Valley. A river winds its way through the southern outskirts of the Parish to join the river Wear a mile or so further east. A main road linking Durham, Lanchester and Consett passes through the older part of the village, forming the main street. About midway along, a road turns off at right angles to Sacriston. The newer part of the village lies on either side of this road and consists of two housing estates built during this century.

The people living here earn their living by travelling to work into neighbouring villages and towns, also into the City of Durham.

No pit heaps scar the rural character of this place chosen 14 centuries ago by our ancestors. The first record of a Norman Overlord was of one Gilbert De La Ley, who lived here from 1120 to 1180. Charters and deeds executed by this man are still preserved in the library of The Dean and Chapter at Durham.

The Leper Hospital, now Holmes' Farm, known as Witton Hall, is the only historic building remaining. It is on the site of the old Leper Hospital of St Mary Magdalene. The oldest part of the farm are the portions that remain of the Leper Hospital, on the gable end, facing the lane, can be seen the head of a two light window which had consisted of two pointed lights within one arch moulding which contains the Ball Ornament.

There was also a lepers' chapel on the slope south of the church near to the river Browney, known as St John's Green. All that is left is a heap of stones. In the 13th and 14th centuries life became prosperous by the processions of Bishops and Prior. Royal visitors came too, among them was King John, Henry II and Edward I.

The purchasing power of money was much greater. Mr Wermuth was glad to sell chickens, one penny each, pigeons three a penny, a kid for two pence, lambs ten pence, a mare for five shillings, sheep varied in price.

The poor could not afford luxuries but they were not badly off for the necessities of life. Wages were good but misused by certain villagers. A Court of Justice at Durham recorded twelve people appearing between 1422 and 1455. Houses were being built by wealthy people. Witton was still a rural village and as wages increased so did prices. Soon the number of very poor people was considerable. It is recorded that six almshouses were built on Front Street. They were pulled down in the 1950s.

There were two charities in the village. The first, dated 1624, was left by Cuthbert Watson. The second was known as The Jane Finney Charity. Income from these charities, amounting to £20 per year, has been used for the assistance of children from the parish who have won places in secondary schools. Old sports included bear baiting, bull fighting, and cock fighting. Executions, which took place at Dryburn, three miles from Witton Gilbert, often served as an excuse for a public holiday. Another source of income was a trading market. Farmers from the Dales brought wool and livestock to trade for coal from the east of the county. There was a Toll House, known as the Gate House, at the bottom of Nor Lane. It was pulled down in the 1950s to make way for the new road. Another toll gate was at the foot of Newton Street. The name of Fad or Fold still persists to describe parts of the village where these markets were held.

Next to Snook Acres Farm, is the old Blacksmith's shop, owned by the Bainbridge family, which still stands today and is a listed building. Built in 1832, the Wesleyan Methodists took over a chapel that had been used by the United Methodists and it is still in service to the village people.

East of Park View was an old Quakers burial ground, somewhere near a private site called Dellaley. Close by, the Colliery Farm still stands empty. Next to the Methodist Chapel there was the old trough or well where spring water was running in. Many a man and beast had a refreshing drink here.

There were six public houses on Front Street. Only two now remain in service – the Travellers Rest and the Glendenning Arms. This had a thatched roof until a gale in 1839 tore off the roof and blew down the

Blacksmith's Shop, Witton Gilbert

chimney stack whilst the landlady Mrs Betty Glendenning was boiling puddings over the fire. She is reputed to have calmly rescued the puddings, cleaned them and served them up to the guests. Alas, they still tasted of soot! In the 19th and 20th centuries rapid development took place. The growing importance of the coal trade resulted in collieries being opened in neighbouring villages. A small drift mine which was opened at the bottom of the slope was known as the Little Pit, owned by Mrs Precod.

There were a few characters in the village. One was old Irish Ann who worked at Witton Hall farm. She worked like a man, all hours, in all weathers. She smoked a clay pipe and got drunk and was prepared to fight any man or woman in the village. Various other characters came into the village to sell their wares. Fish Nellie was one with a big basket of fish which she carried on her head. She came by train from South Shields to Witton Railway Station (now closed). Gypsies came with their goods of buttons, laces, thread, paper flowers, and fortune telling.

In 1862 the railway came from Durham up through the Browney Valley to Consett, Witton Gilbert railway station being a mile from the village.

The Cooper Hall, named in memory of Councillor Harry Cooper MBE JP for his work in the village, is a community centre where various activities take place.

The Women's Institute was formed in 1947. Mrs Martin, President in the 1950s received the MBE for her service to the village, receiving it from Lord Barnard. In the new part of the village you will find the paper shop, fish shop and two grocery shops and the Workmens Club. In the council estate stands Fyndoune House catering for elderly people. Also by the road side on the main road to Sacriston stands the War Memorial to the memory of the men who fell in the First World War.

Witton le Wear

The old village of Witton le Wear lies roughly four miles up river from Bishop Auckland on the edge of the Pennines. Still displaying its medieval street pattern around a village green, the settlement is almost certainly pre-Conquest. The name itself betrays the Saxon roots. Twelfth century *Wudetun*, by then a manor in the gift of the Bishop of Durham, is derived from the Old English *Widu-tun*, literally 'tun (village) by a wood.'

Modified eventually to Witton, the 'le' was a later addition derived from the Old French preposition *lés* (near). 'Wear' is simply Celtic for water. So the name records a succession of conquerors and conquered from the ancient British to the Norman.

It is a Norman knight, one Sir Robert de Amondevill, who first gets Witton into the history books. His name is recorded at the Battle of Lewes, where Henry III and Simon de Montfort fought it out in 1246. Other lords of the manor were to follow and by the late 14th century a castle was built by the great family of Eures, a buccaneering bunch who earned national notoriety when they kidnapped two Italian cardinals in 1317.

By Tudor times, when the border wars with the Scots had virtually ceased, and after pre-Reformation limits on production and despoilation had been abandoned by Elizabeth I, the Eures were to become magnates in iron and coal and continued to prosper well into the 17th century when 'that ancient race fell into female issue.' The castle, which went through a number of hands in the following 300 years, was largely dismantled in the 18th century. Only the curtain wall survives today. The manor's links with the Durham Palatinate, which anyway had been indirect since the time of Henry II, were finally broken after the Civil War when the Bishop's estates were confiscated by Parliament. For centuries the Bishops of Durham had thrived on Weardale mineral wealth, most famously the silver-rich lead ore. Some of this wealth, we may suppose, was channelled through Witton, where a Silver Street once occupied the site of the present Post Office Street.

The wealth increased as industrial production in the County grew throughout the 17th century. At the same time the old families were eclipsed locally as rich yeomen began to appear. The Langstaffs of Witton make their mark about this time. Soon Witton becomes prized for its salubrious air, and well-built houses begin to replace the meaner garths around the green. A grammar school was built in the early 1700s on the site now occupied by The Belfry in Station Road. In the mid-19th century, a little after the railway had reached the village, six new pits had been sunk in the surrounding fields. Now, for the first time in its history, Witton's inhabitants ceased to be predominantly agriculturalists and tradesmen. Miners came down the valley, from Scotland, and from southern counties to win the coal, especially the famous Brockwell, ideally suited to the new art of steel-making. New houses, built in terraces, sprung up near the pit-heads at Marshall Green and across the railway line. The chapel appeared in the same period to 'compassionate' the rough hewers and a little later, a Mechanics Institute was built on the site of the Mason's Arms, now Mr Attle's house in School Street, named after the Board School of the 1870s. At its peak the village boasted three drift mines, five pubs (including an old staging post, The Grey Mare, on the tolled A68), a railway station, six shops, a smithy, a quarry, a hall (the medieval Towers by the West End), two schools, a castle and a mill. The whole supported in 1901 a population of 2,783 souls, a six-fold increase in 100 years. But industrial growth is a fickle thing and when the circus moved on the village contracted again, suddenly less self-sufficient, much of its fabric careworn and its church derelict. It lay waiting for commuterism and a new role.

Index